Plough Quarterly

BREAKING GROUND FOR A RENEW

T0108447

Autumn 2014, Number 2

Artists: *Wassily Kandinsky, Kim Ki-chang, Henri Martin, John Moore, Marc Chagall,
Egon Schiele, Kang Woo-geun, Camille Pissarro, Jason Landsel, Aristarkh Lentulov*

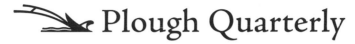

Plough Quarterly

BREAKING GROUND FOR A RENEWED WORLD

www.plough.com

Plough Quarterly features original stories, ideas, and culture to inspire everyday faith and action. Starting from the conviction that the teachings and example of Jesus can transform and renew our world, it aims to apply them to all aspects of life, seeking common ground with all people of goodwill regardless of creed. The goal of *Plough Quarterly* is to build a living network of readers, contributors, and practitioners so that, in the words of Hebrews, we may "spur one another on toward love and good deeds."

Plough Quarterly is published by Plough, the publishing house of the Bruderhof, an international movement of Christian communities whose members are called to follow Jesus together in the spirit of the Sermon on the Mount and of the first church in Jerusalem, sharing all our talents, income, and possessions (Acts 2 and 4). Bruderhof communities, which include both families and single people from a wide range of backgrounds, are located in the United States, England, Germany, Australia, and Paraguay. Visitors are welcome at any time. To learn more about the Bruderhof's faith, history, and daily life, or to find a Bruderhof community near you to arrange a visit, go to *www.bruderhof.com*.

Editors: Peter Mommsen, Sam Hine, Maureen Swinger. Art director: Emily Alexander.
Web editor: Carole Vanderhoof. Contributing editors: Veery Huleatt, Charles Moore, Chungyon Won.

Founding Editor: Eberhard Arnold (1883–1935)

Plough Quarterly No. 2: Building Justice
Published by Plough Publishing House, ISBN 978-0-87486-607-0
Copyright © 2014 by Plough Publishing House. All rights reserved.

All Bible references are taken from the New Revised Standard Version unless otherwise noted.

Christian Wiman's poem "Little Religion" (page 19) appears in his forthcoming collection *Once in the West* (Farrar, Straus and Giroux, 2014). The original German of Maximilian Probst's essay "Heroes: Now It's Your Turn" (page 46) first appeared in *Die Zeit* #30/2013, © Zeitverlag Gerd Bucerius GmbH & Co. KG. The original Korean of Kwon Jeong-saeng's story "The Bell Ringer" (page 52) is copyright © Kwon Jeong-saeng Culture Foundation for Children. The original Korean of the same author's essay "The Church I Dreamed Of" (page 59) was published in *Uridului Haneunim* (Seoul: Green Review, 2008), © Green Review.

Front cover: *Cleaning up Debris in Minutka Square, Grozny*, photograph from RIA Nowosti / AKG-Images. Inside front cover: Painting by Wassily Kandinsky © 2014 Artists Rights Society (ARS), New York / ADAGP, Paris, photograph from AKG-Images. Page 4: Illustrations by Kim Ki-chang © Woonbo Foundation of Culture. Page 32: Painting by Marc Chagall © 2014 Artists Rights Society (ARS), New York / ADAGP, Paris, photograph by Philippe Migeat © CNAC/MNAM/Dist. RMN-Grand Palais / Art Resource, New York. Page 44: Photograph by Luca Galuzzi, *www.galuzzi.it*.

Editorial Office	*Subscriber Services*	*United Kingdom*	*Australia*
PO Box 398	PO Box 345	Brightling Road	4188 Gwydir Highway
Walden, NY 12586	Congers, NY 10920-0345	Robertsbridge	Elsmore, NSW
T: 845.572.3455	T: 800.521.8011	TN32 5DR	2360 Australia
info@plough.com	*subscriptions@plough.com*	T: +44(0)1580.883.344	T: +61(0)2.6723.2213

Plough Quarterly (ISSN 2372-2584) is published quarterly by Plough Publishing House, PO Box 398, Walden, NY 12586.
Individual subscription $32 per year in the United States; Canada add $8, other countries add $16.
Application to mail at periodicals postage pricing is pending at Walden, NY and additional mailing offices.
POSTMASTER: Send address changes to *Plough Quarterly*, PO Box 345, Congers, NY 10920-0345.

Dear Reader,

"Justice" has become a rallying cry for many Christians today. And for good reason: justice is at the heart of the kingdom of God, as Jesus and the Hebrew prophets made abundantly clear.

Yet once our eyes have been opened to the gospel's demand for justice, it's easy to feel overwhelmed. Child poverty, mass incarceration, oppression of women, human trafficking, religious persecution – these and many other evils cry out for redress, making legitimate claims on our conscience. Where is an individual or a church to start?

More fundamentally, what is the nature of the justice we ought to be pursuing? Obviously not all that goes by the name "justice" in our culture is necessarily the justice of God's kingdom. How can we tell the difference?

Jesus teaches us to "seek first the kingdom of God and his righteousness"– or in scholar N.T. Wright's translation, "Make your top priority God's kingdom and his way of life." God's justice, in other words, is not a goal to be achieved through successful projects or viral campaigns. (As Pope Francis has reminded us, the church is not an NGO.) Instead, God's justice is a new life, one that the first Christians called "the Way," a vocation we are to live out every day – first in our life together as the church, and then through our work in the world.

This issue of *Plough Quarterly* explores how to build this kind of justice. In compiling material, we soon realized we'd never manage to be comprehensive; many important topics (for example race, the environment, criminal justice, and war) will have to wait for future issues. All the same, since justice is not merely a vague ideal, this issue addresses a number of concrete questions: wealth and private property, care for the marginalized, marriage and children, restorative justice, and immigration. While our contributors hold diverse views on many subjects, they each cast light from a different angle on how to put God's justice into practice – and challenge us to get started.

As you may know, Plough is much more than a magazine. Many of you will have first encountered us as an online oasis, or as the publisher of books on discipleship and life issues, or as a group of people trying to put Jesus' teachings into practice together (see page 39). For those new to Plough, in these pages we'll be featuring reviews and excerpts of our forthcoming titles, as well as other books we think deserve your attention (pages 66–67).

This autumn we're especially excited about the release of *Their Name Is Today: Reclaiming Childhood in a Hostile World* by much-loved Plough author Johann Christoph Arnold. In fact, we're offering a free advance review copy to every *Plough Quarterly* reader who requests one before November 1, 2014. Interested? See page 8 for details.

As always, we depend on your inspiration, so please keep the responses coming.

Warm greetings

Peter

Peter Mommsen
Editor

We are beyond thrilled, both with the content of the first issue (it is so right to start with the Sermon on the Mount) and with the revival of Plough's magazine. We have been deeply nourished and encouraged over the years by spiritual insights from Plough – we still have every issue from twenty years ago – and I know that we and sojourners like us need the uniquely Christocentric voice that it represents.

Dan and Wendy Ziegler, Haiti

"The Best of Classic Children's Bibles" by Maureen Swinger

This enjoyable article encouraged me to keep reading Bible stories to my children and inspired me to share how my family made our own children's Bible. A few years ago I received a Christmas card from my former teacher in Korea with artwork that fascinated me. It was a nativity scene depicting a cow pen, in which a huge ox stood behind a mother in traditional Korean costume who was holding the baby. Other women dressed similarly greeted the newborn, bringing food on a low table as is the custom in Korea.

Illustrations by Kim Ki-chang from *The Life of Jesus: Collection of Sacred Paintings*

I had long wondered how the Christian faith can be expressed in a genuinely Korean way. Much of what I used to hear and see in church seemed foreign to me, as it had been imported by missionaries. I remember wondering as a child why all the people in the Bible looked like "Western people."

Because the Christmas card was so striking, I began to research the artist, Kim Ki-chang (1913–2001). During the Korean War (1950–1953) he fled to Busan, where he painted twenty-nine pictures of the life of Jesus, depicting Korean garments, houses, and mountains. These illustrations portray the difficulties of the war time and the artist's longing for liberation of body and soul.

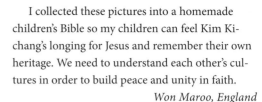

I collected these pictures into a homemade children's Bible so my children can feel Kim Ki-chang's longing for Jesus and remember their own heritage. We need to understand each other's cultures in order to build peace and unity in faith.

Won Maroo, England

"Was Bonhoeffer Willing to Kill?" by Charles Moore

How can you worry about whether Bonhoeffer was willing to kill Hitler when you haven't decided yet what you are willing to do about killing babies?

During my time in Europe I visited Bergen-Belsen, where Anne Frank died. I observed the substantial farm buildings across the road. It was only sixteen years after the war, and I thought about the people there: Can you do nothing while thousands are dying across the road?

I used this observation in a *pro se* defense in Albany Police Court – I was charged with blocking an entrance to an abortion clinic. Our side loved it but the judge didn't, and I got fourteen days. I can remember when anti-war activists made wonderful statements about the evils of nuclear war and got arrested at a missile base every year. We're still waiting for the next nuclear bomb, but we're at more than fifty million abortions and counting.

Jerry Lehmann, New York

We are reading the first *Plough Quarterly* with great interest and tasted it like warm bread with peanut butter. We like the presentation, organization, and art; the articles are serious without being too academic. We also like its intercultural and intergenerational character. While easy to read, it challenges our comfortable middle-class life – the Sermon on the Mount again pushes us to walk against the current.

Hugo and Norma Zorrilla, Pennsylvania

We welcome letters to the editor. Letters and web comments may be edited for length and clarity, and may be published in any medium. Letters should be sent with the writer's name and address to letters@plough.com.

Building Casa de Cristo

In early 2012, the young members of Villa Primavera, the Bruderhof house community in Asunción, Paraguay, dreamed of building a church in the vacant lot next to their house. As an ecumenical place of worship, it was to be called Casa de Cristo – "House of Christ." Johann Blough, age 27, who has worked on the project from the beginning, explains their vision: "Casa de Cristo will be a gathering place for all those in Paraguay – whether neighbors, acquaintances or passers-through – who want to join together in seeking to live out God's kingdom on earth. More than two million people live in the Asunción metropolitan region. At our gatherings on Sundays and in weekday Bible study groups, our wish is to welcome many here who want to follow Jesus' teachings, regardless of church affiliation."

After two years and much toil, this dream is becoming a reality. Community members have worked beside Paraguayan contractors, digging the foundations, laying the bricks, and erecting the beams – all with a minimum of power tools. Neighbors are supportive of the effort, and Blough reports interest from a range of people in the Asunción area. Now, anticipating the opening this fall, a sign outside the building proclaims ¡Bienvenidos! On the beam in the meeting hall is carved the new church's watchword from Philippians: "Rejoice in the Lord always." ⤳

International Fellowship of Reconciliation: One Hundred Years for Nonviolence

On the eve of the First World War, an English Quaker and a German Lutheran bid each other farewell after a peace conference in Constance, Germany, promising never to go war because they were "one in Christ." To honor and build upon this promise, the Fellowship of Reconciliation was founded in England in 1915; the German branch was formed soon afterwards.

After the First World War, a conference in the Netherlands in 1919 established an International Fellowship of Reconciliation (IFOR) from those that had been formed during the war. Over the next years they advocated for disarmament and against the idea of "righteous war." During World War II, they also worked to save people from the Holocaust.

In a 1922 issue, *Plough Quarterly's* forerunner publication *Das Neue Werk* reported on IFOR's development, noting that it grew from "the rock of unity in the living Christ." Thanks to this foundation, the organization has weathered a century of civil wars, genocide, and two world wars. In August 2014, IFOR celebrated its centennial in Constance, one hundred years after a simple handshake gave it birth. ⤳

www.ifor.org

International Fellowship of Reconciliation conference, Bilthoven, Netherlands, October 1919
Photograph courtesy IFOR

From groundwork to completion, Casa de Cristo, Asunción, Paraguay

Sandpile Parenting

Lessons from a Carefree Childhood

JOHANN CHRISTOPH ARNOLD

Every child needs to discover the magic of making snow angels, splashing in puddles, or climbing trees. Parents need to slow down and savor the precious years with the children God has entrusted to them. The years do not come back. Before you know it, your children are adults. The relationship you share then depends on the quality of the time spent together in their earliest memories.

As a child of European refugees who fled to South America during the Second World War, I grew up in the backwoods of Paraguay. My parents raised all seven of us children on the reformer Friedrich Froebel's educational principles, focusing on the importance of play, singing, and storytelling, with the outdoors as our best classroom.

The author as a boy in Paraguay

We had no fancy playgrounds and nothing that could be classified as play equipment. What we did have was a big sandpile and a nearby river where we would entertain ourselves for hours. These places became like friends to us. Here our imaginations could run wild, and we built castles, houses, and any other structures we could dream up. Being mostly outdoors, we discovered insects, plants, and animals.

We were completely satisfied with our adventures, and did not wish for anything more. We had such a great time that often our parents and teachers had difficulty getting us back to do our farm chores, of which there were plenty. In today's modern age, the importance of the sandpile can be rediscovered. If it kept me happy, it can surely keep other children happy!

Someone once gave my family a small monkey for a pet. We named him Berto. He was very lively and affectionate. Berto became a part of our family and would jump on our shoulders as we went on walks. We loved him very much. He had, however, one very bad habit, which our neighbor Martin did not appreciate. Berto always ate up all the tomatoes and other garden plants which Martin planted and nurtured with great care and effort. Although his children also enjoyed the monkey, Martin complained to my father, Heinrich, about Berto's garden thievery. My father had to find a way to get rid of the monkey. One day he asked me to help him return Berto to the wild.

That was a hard day, and we children cried, unable to imagine our family without him. I bravely went along with my father, taking Berto deep into the jungle. When we thought we had walked far enough, my father let him go, and Berto very happily climbed the closest tree. Monkeys are incredibly smart. They can mimic human behavior, such as waving with their paws, laughing, and crying. So as we turned and walked away, Berto waved goodbye to us. We sadly returned to our house.

Upon our return, Berto was waiting for us at the door. He was very happy to see us and waved his arms to welcome us. After we had released him, he must have swung from tree to tree at great speed, to get to our house before we returned. We children laughed and cried for joy, but we also knew he couldn't stay.

After a few days we took Berto back into the jungle. This time we went much further and crossed a river before we released him. We knew that because monkeys cannot swim, this parting would be final, and it would be the last time I could carry him on my shoulder. His departure left a big hole in our family, but gave me a new understanding for the ways of animals, from mimicry to homing instinct, and for the ways of humans, as we learn to

let go of something we love. It also gave me a wonderful story to tell my grandchildren!

Looking back on my childhood, I realize that poverty and disease affected us, and hard physical work was part of daily life. There was no indoor plumbing, no central heating, and, for many years, no electricity. Meals were cooked on an open fire, and there was always wood to split and stack, and water to carry. Grass was cut with a machete; it was coarse, heavy, and high, especially after rainfall. As a teenager, I grumbled about the never-ending chores, but my parents had no pity. And in retrospect I am grateful. I see now how their insistence taught me self-discipline, concentration, perseverance, and the ability to carry through – all things one needs to be a father.

It's important to give children chores and expect them to contribute to the family on a daily basis. That is not the same as scheduling a continuous round of organized sports, clubs, and academics, and robbing them of the time they need to develop on their own.

Granted, children ought to be stretched and intellectually stimulated. They should be taught to articulate their feelings, to write, to read, to develop and defend an idea, to think critically. But what is the purpose of the best academic education if it fails to prepare children for life?

The parental desire to have brilliant children is surely just another sign of our distorted vision – a reflection of the way we tend to view children as little adults. And the best antidote to that is to drop all of our adult expectations entirely, to get down on the same level as our children, to look them in the eye. Only then will we begin to hear what they are saying,

find out what they are thinking, and see the goals we have set for them from their point of view. Only then will we be able to lay aside our own ambitions for them. As poet Jane Tyson Clement writes:

> Child, though I am meant to teach you much,
> what is it, in the end,
> except that together we are
> meant to be children
> of the same Father,
> and I must unlearn
> all the adult structure
> and the cumbering years
> and you must teach me
> to look at the earth and the heaven
> with your fresh wonder.

Johann Christoph Arnold is a senior pastor of Bruderhof communities and co-founder of Breaking the Cycle, a program teaching nonviolent conflict resolution in schools and youth facilities. This article is excerpted from his twelfth book, Their Name Is Today: Reclaiming Childhood in a Hostile World *(Plough, 2014).*

Birding in the Bush

According to naturalist John Burroughs, the key to unlocking the secret riches of the natural world lies in the "capacity to take a hint." I vividly recall a childhood treasure hunt and the thrill of discovery as each new clue was scrutinized until its hidden message was revealed, upon which we all sprinted on to the next hiding place.

Can there be anything more thrilling than embarking on this hunt, one clue at a time? It is, as Rachel Carson writes, "a matter of becoming receptive to what lies around you, learning again to use your eyes, ears, nostrils, and finger tips," of rediscovering as adults the sense of wonder inborn in all children. There is abundant treasure (and challenge) to be found along the way.

Observing birds in their natural setting is a passion that takes me outdoors in every season, into every available habitat. Living in "the bush" of the New South Wales tablelands, I have found that birding presents unique opportunities as well as hazards. I'm not speaking about the deadly spiders and snakes. It's the flies: lots of them.

To combat these pests, I've mastered the "birder's blast." Keeping binoculars poised in both hands, I alternately aim jets of air from the corner of my mouth to each eye and then toward the nostrils, thus depriving the flies of their favorite landing sites. But I must remember to inhale through the nose – otherwise the gulp taken between blasts will simply suck the pesky things down the throat. By the time I've coughed and spluttered and finally swallowed a few, the startled bird has long since flown out of range.

Bill Wiser lives in Elsmore, Australia.

Happily, another bird will come soon enough. And what striking birds they are. Discovering them must have been sheer exhilaration for the first Europeans on this continent, who'd been accustomed to far less color (there are dozens of drab Old World warblers for every brilliant European Goldfinch). Glancing through an Australian bird guide gives you a sense of their excitement – it seems they soon ran out of superlatives when naming all the new species (new to them, that is): consider, for instance, the Lovely, the Splendid, and the Superb Fairy-wren, to name just three of the Maluridae family.

Readers in the northern hemisphere will find zebra finches in most pet stores; here I've met up to twenty-five of these zany little birds lined up on a fence line. The nearby paddocks are graced with five other species whose names are miniature poems: the Diamond Firetail, Chestnut-breasted Mannikin, and Plum-headed, Red-browed, and Double-barred Finches. Binoculars reveal the lovely details of these marvelous creations, each species so unique and yet so finch; a dozen more are found across Australia. They bring to mind another word of Carson's:

> Those who dwell, as scientists or laymen, among the beauties and mysteries of the earth are never alone or weary of life. Whatever the vexations or concerns of their personal lives, their thoughts can find paths that lead to inner contentment and to renewed excitement in living. ⤳

The Splendid and the Superb Fairy-wren

THE GOOD EARTH

FRED BAHNSON

Composting as Prayer

Henri Martin, Cultivation of the Vines

By early May the cover crops would be five feet tall. When the rye reached milk stage and the vetch and clover flowered purple and crimson, I would walk up and down the beds swinging a scythe, the stalks falling before me, the air growing redolent with grassy perfume, and then I would rake up the cuttings to make compost. First the green layer: fresh rye, vetch, and clover stalks. Then a brown layer: old hay or leaves. The third layer would be a dusting of garden soil, containing the spark of bacteria that would set this biological pyre aflame. In a week the tiny hordes inside the compost pile would expend their oxygen, slowing their combustion, and I would turn the pile with a pitchfork to give them air. All kinds of organic matter could go into a compost pile. Once I even composted a dead field rat; a few months later there was nothing but bones.

I love making compost. The bright green of freshly mown grasses; steam arising from the pile on a cold morning; the smell of the forest floor in your hands. There is a secret joy, a kind of charity to be found in this act, transforming a pile of grass and dirt and old leaves into an offering of humic mystery. . . . After several months of heating and cooling and turning, the pile of well-cooked humus would be ready to spread onto the soil. Into that I would plant Speckled Trout lettuce, Kuri squash, or Sugarsnap peas, which would feed the hungry people of Cedar Grove. The people's hunger could be slackened, but all the while the secret life of soil would continue, the gift waiting to be found. Like a ceaseless hymn of praise, this cycle went on with or without you, winter and summer, rain and drought, seedtime and harvest, a process of creating beyond your control that had been in motion since the foundation of the world.

Fred Bahnson is a permaculture gardener and the director of the Food, Faith, and Religious Leadership Initiative at Wake Forest University School of Divinity. He lives with his wife Elizabeth and their three sons in North Carolina. Taken from Fred Bahnson's Soil and Sacrament: A Spiritual Memoir of Food and Faith *(Simon and Schuster, 2013).*

We're All Adopted

Why Orphans Are at the Heart of the Gospel

KRISH KANDIAH

On August 31, 1939, the order to "evacuate forthwith" sounded over Britain's radios, sending nearly three million children away from their homes and families. Code-named "Operation Pied Piper" and planned in anticipation of Nazi air raids, this huge evacuation moved children and others from high-risk urban areas to the safer countryside and overseas. Four days later Britain declared war on Germany and World War II began. This year marks Operation Pied Piper's seventy-fifth anniversary.

As they boarded trains travelling out of their home cities, the children did not know if they would ever see their parents again. Yet on reaching the countryside, they were received by families who opened their homes, often at considerable sacrifice. For many from poor inner-city homes, it was their first experience of a healthy, well-nourished life.

> Learn to do good;
> seek justice,
> rescue the oppressed,
> defend the orphan,
> plead for the widow.
> *Isaiah 1:17*

Three quarters of a century later, we must rediscover the welcoming generosity of Operation Pied Piper. We do not face air raids, but today there are thousands of children who need homes and families. In England alone there are six thousand children waiting for adoption, and another eighty-six hundred need foster care. In 1939, even men and women who could scarcely afford it welcomed children – many from difficult backgrounds – into their homes. We need that spirit today.

Christians have another reason to welcome these children. Throughout scripture, God – called the "father to the fatherless" and the "protector of widows and orphans" – has a special concern for the vulnerable. When Jesus' brother teaches us that our faith is only "pure and unde-filed" if we "visit orphans and widows in their affliction" (James 1:27), he is merely underlining what prophets like Isaiah already taught.

Earlier this year I spoke at a London-wide gathering of one hundred senior social workers. I asked the assembled group to name the challenges they face when working with Christians. The suspected problems – Christian views on "same-sex couples" and "proselytism" – came up.

Then I asked the social workers to think of the advantages of working with the church. "Great support network for adopters," they said. "Altruistic motives," they added, and "genuinely diverse communities." It was encouraging to see a secular gathering recognize the role that the church can play for vulnerable children.

But then I explained the most compelling reason for churches to engage with this subject: adoption is a core part of the Christian story. Every Christian is an adopted person; we have all been adopted into God's family. Paul wrote in his letter to the Romans:

> For you did not receive a spirit of slavery to fall back into fear, but you have received a spirit of adoption. When we cry, "Abba! Father!" it is that very Spirit bearing witness with our spirit that we are children of God, and if children, then heirs, heirs of God and joint heirs with Christ. (Romans 8:15–17)

I pray that the spirit of the 1939 evacuation might again capture our society's imagination, and that the "spirit of adoption" will capture the church's heart.

Krish Kandiah is president of the London School of Theology and founder and director of Home for Good, a foster care and adoption ministry.

The Economy of the Early Church

Why the Christians Abandoned Private Property

EBERHARD ARNOLD

Jesus brought a fresh, new message to the world. It is a message that heralds both judgment and rebirth. It announces a totally different social order: the coming reign of God, which will bring to an end the present age ruled by man. Without God we sink down into hollowness and coldness of heart, into stubbornness and self-delusion. In Jesus the Father revealed his love to us, a love that wants to conquer and rule everything that once belonged to it. Jesus calls, urging a divided humankind to sit together at one table, God's table, where there is room for all. He invites all people to a meal of fellowship and fetches his guests from the roadsides and skid rows. The future age comes as God's banquet, God's wedding-feast, God's reign of unity. God will be Lord over his creation again, consummating the victory of his spirit of unity and love. . . .

The new future puts an end to all powers, legal systems, and property laws now in force. The coming kingdom reveals itself even now wherever

Mark 1:14–15

Luke 14:15–24

Rev. 19:1–10

God's all-powerful love unites people in a life of surrendered brother-hood. Jesus proclaimed and brought nothing but God, nothing but his coming rule and order. He founded neither churches nor sects. His life belonged to greater things. Pointing toward the ultimate goal, he gave the direction. He brought us God's compass, which determines the way by taking its bearings from the pole of the future.

John 14:6

Jesus called people to a practical way of loving brotherhood. This is the only way in keeping with our expectation of that which is coming. It alone leads us to others, it alone breaks down the barriers erected by the covetous will to possess, because it is determined to give itself to all. The Sermon on the Mount depicts the liberating power of God's love wherever it rules supreme. When Jesus sent out his disciples and ambassadors, he gave them their work assignment, without which no one can live as he did: in word and deed we are to proclaim the imminence of the kingdom. He gives authority to overcome diseases and demonic powers. To oppose the order of the present world epoch and focus on the task at hand we must abandon all possessions and take to the road. The hallmark of his mission is readiness to become a target for people's hatred in the fierce battle of spirits, and finally, to be killed in action.

Matt. 5–7

Matt. 10

After Jesus was killed the small band of his disciples in Jerusalem proclaimed that though their leader had been shamefully executed, he was indeed still alive and remained their hope and faith as the bringer of

Sheep grazing on the Judean Hills

This groundbreaking essay, first published in 1926 to introduce a collection of early Christian writings, appears here as the second in a series featuring German theologian and educator Eberhard Arnold (1883–1935). For more on Arnold, including Jürgen Moltmann's "Who Is Eberhard Arnold?", see our first issue or visit www.plough.com. *From* The Early Christians *(Plough, 2014).*

Acts 2–4

the kingdom. The present age, they said, was nearing its end. Humankind was now faced with the greatest turning point ever in its history, and Jesus would appear a second time in glory and authority. God's rule over the whole earth would be ensured.

The powers of this future kingdom could already be seen at work in the early church. People were transformed and made new. The strength to die inherent in Jesus' sacrifice led them to heroically accept the way of *Acts 6:8—7:60* martyrdom, and more, it assured them of victory over demonic powers *Acts 8:4–8* of wickedness and disease. He who rose to life through the Spirit had a strength that exploded in an utterly new attitude to life: love to one's brother and love to one's enemy, the divine justice of the coming kingdom. Through this new spirit, property was abolished in the early church. Material possessions were handed over to the ambassadors for the poor *Acts 11:27–30* of the church. Through the presence and power of the Spirit and through faith in the Messiah, this band of followers became a brotherhood.

This was their immense task: to challenge the people of Israel in the face of imminent catastrophe, and more, to shake the whole of humankind from its sleep in the face of certain destruction, so that all might prepare for the coming of the kingdom. The poorest people suddenly knew that their new faith was the determining factor, the decisive moment in the history of humankind. For this tremendous certainty, the early church gained strength in daily reading of the Jewish Law and Prophets; in baptism, the symbol of faith given by the prophet John and Jesus himself to represent submitting to death in a watery grave in order to be reborn; in communal meals celebrated to proclaim the death of Jesus; and in collective prayer to God and Christ. The words and stories of Jesus and all that they demanded were told over and over again. Thus the original sources for the Gospels and New Testament are to be found in *1 Cor. 15:1–8* the early church.

"Lord, come!" was their age-old cry of faith and infinite longing, *1 Cor. 16:22* preserved in the original Aramaic from this early time of first love. He who was executed and buried was not dead. He drew near as the sovereign living one. The Messiah Jesus rose from the dead and his kingdom will break in at his second coming! That was the message of his first followers, such as Peter, who led the church at Jerusalem at its founding.

The spirit of Christ translates love of God into divine service of love to others. Whoever serves the poor, the destitute, the downtrodden, serves *Matt. 25:40* Christ himself, for God is near to them. To be loved by God means to love

God and one's neighbor: community with God becomes community with one another. So out of the expectation of the coming kingdom, life and service in the church take shape. Faith in that which is coming unites the believers in one common will and brings about brotherhood. This bond of unity in common dedication is the positive result of opposition to the present age.

1 John 4:19–21

Such uniting in the Spirit needs no set forms. In the first period, the elders and deacons needed for each community retained the tasks allotted to them, but also accepted the gifts of grace given by the Spirit. Although the tireless travels of the apostles and prophets helped to strengthen the unity between the communities, the consciousness of being one was created solely by the one God, one Lord, one Spirit, one faith, one baptism, one body and soul given to all.

Eph. 4:3–6

Through the Spirit, this oneness resulted in an equality that had its roots in God alone. Just as alienation from God is common to all, so the Spirit bestows his divine gift equally and totally on all. Those gripped by God see all inequality as a powerful incentive to become brothers and sisters in perfect love.[1] The early Christians, united in purpose through the one Spirit, were "brothers" and "sisters" because they were all "consecrated ones," "saints," "the elect," and "believers." The same neediness, guilt, and smallness made them all "poor," a name frequently used for them in the earliest times because their belief in God and their attitude to temporal goods was regarded as poverty.[2]

The freedom to work voluntarily and the possibility of putting one's capabilities to use were the basis for all acts of love and charity. Self-determination in their work gave an entirely voluntary character to all social work done by the early Christians. Hermas gives another indication of the spirit ruling in the church. He writes that the wealthy could be fitted into the building of the church only after they had stripped themselves of their wealth for the sake of their poorer brothers and sisters.[3] Wealth was regarded as deadly to the owner and had to be made serviceable to

---

1. According to the *Didache* (ca. 60–110 AD): "You shall not turn away from someone in need, but shall share everything with your brother or sister, and do not claim that anything is your own. For if you are sharers in what is imperishable, how much more so in perishable things! . . . 'Let your gift sweat in your hands until you know to whom to give it.'" *Didache* 4.8, 1.5–6, trans. Michael W. Holmes in *The Apostolic Fathers* (Baker, 2007).

2. See Adolf von Harnack, *The Mission and Expansion of Christianity in the First Three Centuries*, vol. 1, trans. James Moffat (Harper, 1962), 401 ff.

3. *The Shepherd of Hermas* 6.5–7.

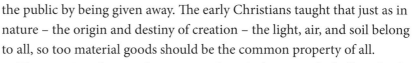

the public by being given away. The early Christians taught that just as in nature – the origin and destiny of creation – the light, air, and soil belong to all, so too material goods should be the common property of all.

The practice of surrendering everything in love was the hallmark of the Christians. When this declined, it was seen as a loss of the spirit of Christ. Urged by this love, many even sold themselves into slavery or went to debtors' prison for the sake of others. Nothing was too costly for the Christians when the common interest of their brotherhood was at stake; they developed an incredible activity in the works of love.[4]

John 13:5

In fact, everything the church owned at that time belonged to the poor. The affairs of the poor were the affairs of the church; every gathering served to support bereft women and children, the sick, and the destitute.[5] The basic feature of the movement, a spirit of boundless voluntary giving, was more essential than the resulting communal life and the rejection of private property. In the early church the spontaneity of genuine love merged private property into a communism of love. This same urge of love later made Christian women of rank give away their property and become beggars. The pagans deplored the fact that instead of commanding respect by means of their wealth, these women became truly pitiful creatures, knocking at doors of houses much less respected than their own had been.[6] To help others, the Christians took the hardest privations upon themselves. Nor did they limit their works of love to fellow believers.[7] Even Emperor Julian had to admit that "the godless Galileans feed our poor in addition to their own."[8]

2 Cor. 8:1–15

According to Christians, the private ownership of property sprang from the primordial sin of man: it was the result of covetous sin. However necessary property might be for life in the present demonic epoch, the Christian could not cling to it. The private larder or storeroom had to be put at the disposal of guests and wanderers just as much as the common treasury.[9] Nor could anybody evade the obligation to extend hospitality. In this way each congregation reached out far beyond its own community.

1 Tim. 6:6–10

But in other ways too the communities helped their brothers and sisters in different places. In very early times the church at Rome enjoyed

4. The pagan Lucian describes the help Christians gave to prisoners in *Peregrinus* 13.

5. Justin Martyr, *First Apology* 67.

6. Macarius Magnes, *Apocriticus* III.5; Porphyry Fragment No. 58 in Harnack's edition, 82. See Harnack, *Mission and Expansion*, vol. 2, 74–75.

7. *Didascalia Apostolorum* XV.

8. Sozomen, *Ecclesiastical History*, V.17; see also Harnack, op. cit, vol. 1, 162.

9. Tertullian, *To His Wife* II.4.

NO POSTAGE
NECESSARY
IF MAILED
IN THE
UNITED STATES

high esteem in all Christian circles because it "presided in works of love."[10] The rich capital city was able to send help in all directions, whereas the poorer Jerusalem had to accept support from other churches in order to meet the needs of the crowds of pilgrims that thronged its streets. Within its own city, the relatively small church at Rome gave regular support to fifteen hundred distressed persons in the year AD 250.[11]

Even in the smallest church community, the overseer had to be a friend of the poor,[12] and there was at least one widow responsible to see to it, day and night, that no sick or needy person was neglected.[13] The deacon was responsible to find and help the poor and to impress on the rich the need to do their utmost. Deacons also served at table. There was no excuse for anyone because he had not learned or was unable to do this service.[14] Everybody was expected to go street by street, looking for the poorest dwellings of strangers. As a result, Christians spent more money in the streets than the followers of other religions spent in their temples.[15] Working for the destitute was a distinguishing mark of the first Christians.

Everyone was equally respected, equally judged, and equally called. The result was equality and fellowship in everything: the same rights, the same obligation to work, and the same opportunities. All this led to a preference for a simple standard of living. Even the spirit-bearers and leaders who were cared for by the church could not expect any more than the simplest fare of the poor. The mutual respect among these early Christians bore fruit in a "socialistic" solidarity rooted in a love that sprang from the belief that all people are born equal.

The rank afforded by property and profession is incompatible with such fellowship and simplicity, and repugnant to it. For that reason alone, the early Christians had an aversion to any high judicial position or commission in the army.[16] They found it impossible to take responsibility for any penalty or imprisonment, any disfranchisement, any judgment

James 2:1–13

---

10. Ignatius of Antioch, *Letter to the Romans,* preamble.

11. Bishop Cornelius, quoted in Eusebius, *Church History* VI.43.11.

12. Tertullian, loc. cit.

13. Harnack, *Texte und Untersuchungen* II (Harnack and Gebhardt, 1886), 24.

14. See Cyprian, *Letters,* especially Letter 62, in *Ante-Nicene Fathers,* vol. 5, ed. A. C. Coxe (Eerdmans, 1952), 355–356.

15. Tertullian, loc. cit.

16. According to Tertullian, one could agree to a Christian's right to hold a high office in which he was empowered to adjudicate over the civic rights of a person only if he did not condemn or penalize anyone, or cause anyone to be put into chains, thrown into prison, or tortured (*On Idolatry* 17).

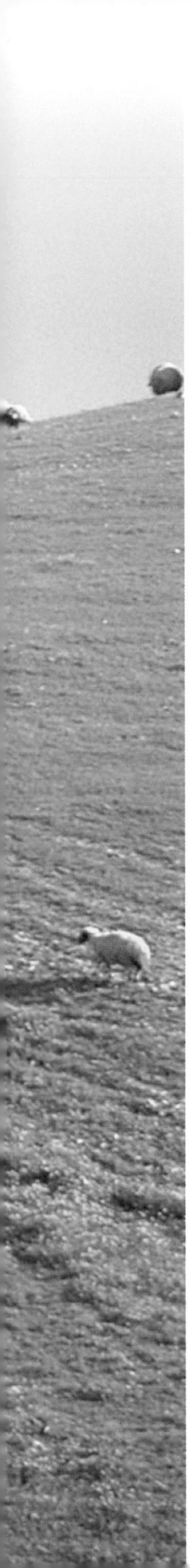

over life or death, or the execution of any death sentence pronounced by martial or criminal courts. Other trades and professions were out of the question because they were connected with idolatry or immorality. Christians therefore had to be prepared to give up their occupations. The resulting unemployment and threat of hunger would be no more frightening than violent death by martyrdom.[17]

James 1:26–27

Underpinning these practical consequences was unity of word and deed. A pattern of daily life emerged that was consistent with the message that the Christians proclaimed. Most astounding to the outside observer was the extent to which poverty was overcome in the vicinity of the communities, through voluntary works of love. It had nothing to do with the more or less compulsory social welfare of the state.

Heb. 13:4

Chastity before marriage, absolute faithfulness in marriage, and strict monogamy were equally tangible changes. In the beginning this was expressed most clearly in the demand that brothers in responsible positions should have only one wife. The foundation for Christian marriage was purely religious: marriage was seen as a symbol of the relationship of the one God with his one people, the one Christ with his one church.

1 Tim. 3:2

Eph. 5:22–33

Eph. 2:15–16

From then on, a completely different humanity was in the making. This shows itself most clearly in the religious foundation of the family, which is the starting point of every society and fellowship, and in the movement toward a communism of love, which is the predominant tendency of all creation. The new people, called out and set apart by God, are deeply linked to the coming revolution and renewal of the whole moral and social order. It is a question of the most powerful affirmation of the earth and humankind. Through their Creator and his miraculous power, the believers expect the perfection of social and moral conditions. This is the most positive attitude imaginable: they expect God's perfect love to become manifest for all people, comprehensively and universally, answering their physical needs as well as the need of their souls.

---

17. Tertullian, *On Idolatry* 12: "Faith does not fear hunger." See Harnack, *Texte und Untersuchungen,* vol. 42, 2 and 4, pp. 117f.).

Little Religion

His little religion
of common things
uncommonly loved
served him well.
Especially in Hell.

*

When the sickbed sunlight
banishes shadows
like the noontime tin
of the storm cellar door
long, long before,
he is the blaze
it takes a man to raise,
he is the stone-
stepped dark a child
goes feelingly down.

*

As if to be
were to be
by oblivion
given
and forgiven
heaven.

CHRISTIAN WIMAN

Liberate Your Wealth

Basil the Great

Theophanes the Greek (ca.1340–1410), *Icon of Saint Basil the Great*

Fling wide your doors! Give your wealth free passage everywhere! As a great river flows by a thousand channels through fertile country, so let your wealth run through many conduits to the homes of the poor. Wells that are drawn from flow the better; left unused, they go foul. . . . Money kept standing idle is worthless, but moving and changing hands it benefits the community and brings increase.

"I am wronging no one," you say, "I am merely holding on to what is mine." What is yours? Who gave it to you so that you could bring it into life with you? Why, you are like a man who pinches a seat at the theater at the expense of latecomers, claiming ownership of what was for common use. That's what the rich are like; having seized what belongs to all they claim it as their own on the basis of having got there first. Whereas if everyone took for himself enough to meet his immediate needs and released the rest for those in need of it, there would be no rich and no poor.

When a man strips another of his clothes, he is called a thief. Should not a man who has the power to clothe the naked but does not do so be called the same? The bread in your larder belongs to the hungry. The cloak in your wardrobe belongs to the naked. The shoes you allow to rot belong to the barefoot. The money in your vaults belongs to the destitute. You do injustice to every person whom you could help but do not.

I ask, "Why do you have all this wealth?" For the care of the poor consumes wealth. When each one receives a little for one's needs, and when all owners distribute their means simultaneously for the care of the needy, no one will possess more than one's neighbor. Yet it is plain that you have much land. Where did it come from? Undoubtedly you have subordinated the relief and comfort of many to your convenience. And so, the more you abound in your riches, the more you want in love.

Basil the Great (ca. AD 330–379), bishop of Caesarea (now Kayseri, Turkey), gave away all he owned and urged wealthy Christians to do the same. He founded a hospital and other social services for the city's poor.

Private property is not a matter of justice, for it is not according to nature, which has brought forth all good things for all in common. God has created everything in such a way that all things are to be possessed in common. Nature therefore is the mother of common right, usurpation the mother of private right.

It is not from your own property that you give to the poor. Rather, you make return from what is theirs. For what has been given as common for the use of all, you have appropriated to yourself alone. The earth belongs to all, not to the rich. Therefore you are paying a debt, not bestowing a gift.

How far, O you rich, do you push your mad desires? "Shall you alone dwell upon the earth?" (Isa. 5:8) The earth was made in common for all. . . . Why do you arrogate to yourselves, you rich, an exclusive right to the soil? Nature, which begets all people as poor, cannot recognize the rich. For we are neither born with raiment nor begotten with gold and silver. Naked the earth brings people into the light, in need of food, clothing, and drink; naked the earth receives those whom it has brought forth; it does not know how to include the boundaries of an estate in a tomb.

"He scattered abroad and gave to the poor, his justice endures forever" (2 Cor. 9:9). . . . This mercy, therefore, is called justice because the giver knows that God has given all things to all in common – that the sun rises for all, his rain falls on all, and he has given the earth for all. On that account the giver shares with those who do not have the abundance of the earth. . . . They are just, therefore, who do not retain anything for themselves alone, knowing that everything has been given to all. ➺

Share All Things in Common
Ambrose of Milan

Late antique mosaic in the church of St. Ambrogio, Milan.

Born into a Roman Christian family, Aurelius Ambrosius (ca. AD 340–397) began a career in public service before being elected bishop of Milan. At first Ambrose fled into hiding, but then accepted service in the church as God's calling, received baptism, and renounced his family wealth. —Excerpts from Ambrose and Basil are taken from Charles Avila, Ownership: Early Christian Teaching *(Orbis, 1983).*

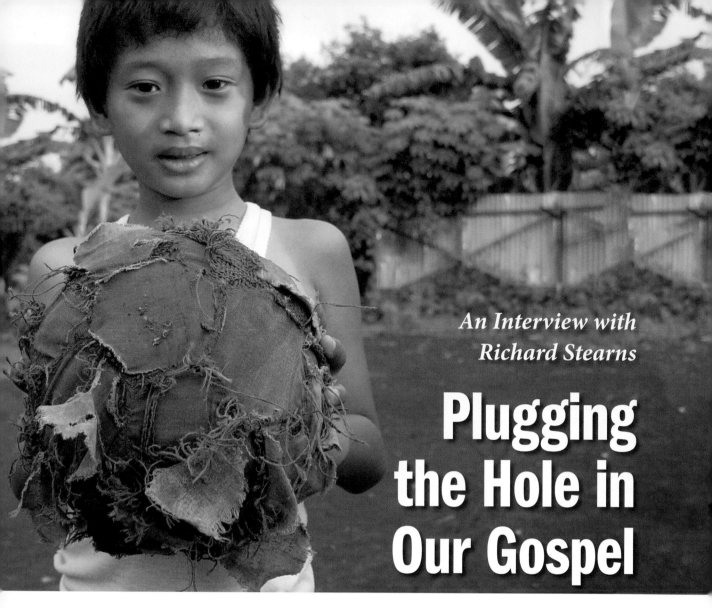

An Interview with
Richard Stearns

Plugging the Hole in Our Gospel

On Killing the American Dream

Richard Stearns is president of World Vision United States and the father of five.

Plough: *This year saw publication of your book* Unfinished: Filling the Hole in Our Gospel. *What is the hole in our gospel?*

Richard Stearns: The gospel is not just good news about personal salvation – it is that, certainly, but it's so much more! At the beginning of the Gospel of Luke, when Jesus gave one of his first public statements, he read from

Isaiah – something which served as a mission statement for him:

> The Spirit of the Lord is on me, because he has anointed me to proclaim good news to the poor. He has sent me to proclaim freedom for the prisoners and recovery of sight for the blind, to set the oppressed free, to proclaim the year of the Lord's favor.

Plough Quarterly • Autumn 2014

The gospel is about justice and compassion; it's about the year of jubilee where debts are forgiven and where economic justice is established. If we don't carry out the whole mission that Christ gave his church, then our gospel has a hole in it.

Jesus blesses the poor but has stern words for the rich, leading you to write that the gospel involves "killing the American dream." What kind of poverty do you see among Western Christians, who are rich compared to billions around the world?

Americans who visit World Vision projects in Africa or South Asia are often disarmed and surprised to see how the poor are so often filled with joy. Children who are destitute are happy playing with a soccer ball made of plastic bags, twine, and scrap paper. Meanwhile our own children are sorely disappointed on Christmas morning if they don't find the iPhone they want under the tree.

The poorest of the poor are often rich in faith – and rich in joy, gratitude, courage, endurance, dependence upon God, and community. Those are the things that we Americans often lack. When you have nothing, God becomes everything. But in North America, God has to compete for our devotion.

World Vision seeks to combat poverty around the globe. Yet in focusing on world poverty, do we risk overlooking our closest neighbors? Martin Luther King Jr., in a reflection on the parable of the Good Samaritan, once quipped that the priest and the Levite who passed by the wounded man as he lay by the road to Jericho were probably going to a meeting of the Jericho Road Improvement Association.

There's a lot of truth to King's observation. I often notice that we Americans are far more eager to help people in Africa than those in our own country. When the poor are distant from us geographically and culturally, we don't feel threatened – we can sponsor a child or make a donation, all at a safe remove. It's different when the poor live right down the street.

Why are we threatened? Perhaps it's because our comfort is called into question by the disparity in resources and the cultural divide that separates us from our poor neighbors. We're not sure how to respond to the homeless person holding a sign. In addition, we're often judgmental, more so than we are toward the poor in the Congo or Angola. If you're poor in America, it's assumed that the reason is laziness, bad choices, alcohol, or drugs.

Yet in the parable of the Good Samaritan, Jesus doesn't tell us why the man was beaten and left by the side of the road. Maybe he was a drug dealer and a deal went bad; maybe he made the ill-advised choice to travel after dark. Jesus just tells us to respond in compassion regardless of why someone is in need.

You've written that Jesus left us three great commandments. The first two are familiar – to love God and to love neighbor. But the third is often forgotten: the Great Commission, where Jesus commands us, to "proclaim the good news to the whole creation" (Mark 16:15). What does this look like?

To understand the Great Commission, we first have to pose the question: Why did Jesus leave? This is a profound question when you think about it. Jesus gave his disciples an assignment to go into the world and make disciples. He tells them: I will return when the assignment is completed. Every follower of Christ is thus his ambassador to proclaim the good news of the coming of the kingdom of God. By loving God, loving our neighbors, and through our actions we are to show the world a different way to live.

According to the Sermon on the Mount, this means living together in community in a way that is radically different from the rest of the world. Church communities are to be outposts of the kingdom of God.

The earliest churches in the Roman Empire were all fledgling little communities of people whose lives were uniquely different from the culture around them. They cared for the poor, loved one another, and were known for their kindness, gentleness, meekness, joy, self-sacrifice, and compassion. As a result, these communities became attractive, like points of light in a dark world. This is what fueled the growth of the church – people said, "Whatever the Christians have, I want it too." It should be just the same today.

What do you say to those who criticize Christian mission as cultural imperialism?

Proclaiming the gospel isn't imperialism, because our job is not to convert people. We are to invite them to experience the forgiveness of their sins and to join the caring community that is the church. But the choice is up to them. If we go to Pakistan or Indonesia proclaiming the coming of the kingdom, we're simply offering the people an opportunity to hear and to respond.

In light of the Great Commission, what is our responsibility as Christians in the public square?

As followers of Jesus, we are called to be salt and light – to form communities that are attractive, winning people to Christ through our lives of love and truth. We're not called to shake a finger at non-believers or to coerce them to be like us.

Paul tells us: "What have I to do with judging those outside? Is it not those who are inside that you are to judge? God will judge those outside" (1 Cor. 5:12-13). Our task is to be an embassy of the love of Christ (2 Cor. 5:20). Only when people are won to Christ will they want to live according to Christian principles.

At times Christians can't avoid the political, as you experienced during the media firestorm last March when World Vision's board amended its policies to recognize civil marriages between employees of the same sex. Two days later, your board reversed that decision. What are your reflections on that now?

I've thought about it a great deal. First, World Vision never altered its view that marriage is a covenant between a man and a woman. In fact, we stated clearly that we were not endorsing same-sex unions. What we attempted to do was find a way to recognize the sad reality of a divided church. As a multi-denominational organization, World Vision includes employees from many different denominations, some of which sanction same-sex relationships as marriage. We drew the analogy that since we don't disqualify someone from employment at World Vision if he or she gets divorced, the same principle should apply with same-sex unions.

But this was a mistake, one for which we have apologized. Unfortunately, by deferring to a few denominations – which are not the majority of our supporters – we effectively let them publicly define us and our belief about marriage. As a result, we ended up revising our employee-conduct policy in a way that was inconsistent with our deeply held beliefs, and this sent a very confusing message. As soon as we recognized our mistake, within about forty-eight hours, we sought to correct it by reversing the change and reiterating our belief in what scripture teaches about marriage.

This unfortunate series of events caused a great deal of uncertainty about who we were and what we believed. That wasn't our intent – we were actually trying to find a way to unite as Christians around our mission to serve the poor. But we did it in a clumsy way, and it was not a good decision. We asked for forgiveness and apologized. All of us on the board offered to resign, but were asked to stay on.

As a result of this controversy, many people cancelled their child sponsorships. Do all the children affected have sponsors again?

When we reversed the decision, it did succeed in stopping the bleeding. In the end, roughly 1.5 percent of our child sponsors walked away from us – not fifty percent, fortunately. Nonetheless, that still means we lost thousands of sponsors for children who can least afford it, and we're faced with the challenge of making up the difference. We're moving forward now, continuing to do the work we've done for more than sixty years, trusting in God for his help.

What challenges can you leave us with, especially those of us who can't go to places of extreme poverty?

First and foremost, every follower of Christ needs to understand clearly why he or she is here. We're not on this earth just for raising our families and enjoying life. We have a mission and a calling. Every morning when we wake up we should be thinking: How can I serve Christ and his cause today, where I am, with the full commitment of my life?

We are like enlisted soldiers on an assignment, and we can't go AWOL. Not all of us are called to sell everything we have and move to the Congo to help the poor (though some of us are). But we should all be living faithful and productive lives for Christ right where we're planted. For some it might be bringing a meal to a shut-in. For others, it might be visiting a nursing home to read to the elderly or just sit and keep them company. It might be to volunteer at your church. There are so many ways that we can be the hands and feet of Christ in our world.

In my book, I describe this as "spiritual dominoes." Think of yourself as a domino that Christ has placed strategically with a critical role to play. All he asks is that we're willing to do the thing we're called to do where he's placed us to do it. When we're faithful in that task, God creates spectacular chain reactions that change the world in really profound ways.

In the 1800s there lived a man named Ed Kimball. All he did was teach Sunday school to a group of teenage boys every week. One of those boys was Dwight L. Moody, who became the greatest evangelist of the nineteenth century. From Moody there was a direct domino effect through several other men leading to the conversion of Billy Graham in the late 1930s. It all began because Ed Kimball showed up and taught Sunday school every Sunday. Kimball never did anything spectacular, but God used his faithfulness. And so there is no such thing as an insignificant follower of Christ. What we do – what God has entrusted us with – has the power to change the world.

Interview by Andrew Zimmerman on July 18, 2014. Listen to the audio version on www.plough.com.

When Love Demands Justice

A Christian Response to America's Immigration Crisis

NOEL CASTELLANOS

Above, US agents take undocumented immigrants into custody near the Texas-Mexico border, July 2014.

Thirty-five years ago I graduated from college and began a vocation of full-time Christian ministry, eager to reach non-religious young people with the love of Christ. After learning from Dr. John Perkins about his biblically informed philosophy of Christian community development, I felt compelled to move my young family from northern California to inner-city Chicago to minister in a Mexican barrio called La Villita ("Little Village"). There I had the privilege of helping to establish a church committed to Perkins' vision.

Chicago is an unlikely place for Mexican immigrants to settle, with its extreme cold and long winters. But it has been a landing point for immigrants from south of the border ever since the end of the bracero program in 1964.

Noel Castellanos, a third-generation Mexican-American, is CEO of the Christian Community Development Association (CCDA), a movement of over five hundred churches and organizations committed to transforming communities by living and working among the poor. www.ccda.org

Created by Congress during World War II, this program aimed to address the nation's shortage of manual labor. By the war's end, seventy-five thousand braceros (manual laborers) were working in the US railroad industry, with over fifty thousand in agriculture.

In the following years, the growth of Mexican labor in the United States exploded, soon drawing heated criticism. As a result, in 1954 over a million Mexican workers were deported in an action called Operation Wetback. Still, by the time the bracero program officially ended, more than half a million Mexicans had legally entered our country to work. Many of these stayed on in the United States without legal status. The government mostly turned a blind eye, since much of our economy continued to depend on cheap Mexican labor.

Even though these workers played a needed role, they suffered harsh discrimination. In Texas, where I was born, Mexicans – like African-Americans – endured "white only" bathrooms and segregated lunch counters as well as deplorable living and working conditions. Though my parents were both born in the United States, they worked as farmhands and in low-paying factory jobs. One of my most vivid childhood memories is of being warned by my grandfather – a Mexican native who became a legal United States resident after crossing the border with his family – to beware of mistreatment from the *bolillos,* a slang word for gringos.

As we started our church and got to know our neighbors in La Villita, I was reminded of my grandmother Juanita. Upon reaching retirement age, she asked one of my uncles to take her to the Social Security Administration offices in Weslaco to figure out what benefits she was entitled to. After looking up her Social Security number, the agent came back with bad news. "We have no record of you ever working or paying into the system." Her response was quick and furious. *"¿Como que no he trabajado?* What do you mean I have never worked? I have worked at home every day raising nine children and taking care of my family!"

The same could be said of many of my friends in La Villita – they work extremely hard every day, and often receive little in return.

It was hard not to be inspired by Leticia. When I met her, I was impressed by her dignity and her determination to provide for her family. On Sunday mornings she was always on time for our church service, even though she often walked a mile in the rain or snow with her kids to get there. Her daughters and son were always the best-dressed children at church with their frilly lace and stylish tie. As I got to know Leticia, I found out she was an entrepreneur: she made and sold tamales, working herself to exhaustion to provide for her kids just as my grandmother had done. Leticia would wake up every day long before the roosters in our barrio began to crow, and would prepare the *pollo, puerco,* and *masa* she needed for the tamales. By 5:00 a.m. she would be out on 31st Street in her designated spot to provide her delicious food to the men and women heading out to work in factories, restaurants, and hotels. Even the day laborers

> **Instead of focusing our efforts in poor communities primarily on pulling drowning people out of the river, we need to go upstream to find out who is pushing them into the water in the first place.**

who gathered at the Home Depot, praying to be picked up for a job, stopped to buy their breakfast from her. After she sold every last tamale, she rushed home in time to dress her children and send them off to school.

Hard-working men and women like Leticia are the most valuable asset in our immigrant community. Yet despite all the sweat and effort my neighbors invest, they seem to barely get by. Often, parents are forced to leave their teenagers unattended for hours as they work double shifts to make ends meet. In too many cases this leads to mischief and gang involvement.

As a church, we felt we had to try to stop this sad pattern. Whenever we spoke to parents about their aspirations, they would inevitably talk to us about their children – like all parents, they wanted a better life for their kids and were willing to sacrifice their own needs and wants to make this happen. Accordingly, our church decided to focus our efforts on investing in children and young people. I was convinced that with the work ethic that existed in our community, we could create better-paying jobs, get young people into college, provide families with opportunities for homeownership, and help our neighbors find authentic faith in Jesus Christ.

In the first few years, we seemed to be on the right track. Our church membership grew, with an influx of barrio residents who were committed to loving their neighbors and being a witness for Christ in the community. We had programs to combat gang violence and to reach the youth. We offered small business loans to our members, and started a homeownership program. We launched educational and summer programs for kids. Lives were being healed and transformed.

Yet as time went on, I began to notice that there was something missing in our work of Christian community development – a gap that threatened any success our efforts might have.

My friend Fernando was always working, and always seemed to be looking for a better job. I found out that back home in Mexico he had studied civil engineering. Here in the United States he worked in low-wage construction jobs to feed his family. He was eager to grow in his faith, and often stopped by my house or the church office to talk. The more I found out about his life, the more I realized the godlike power our nation's immigration system wielded over his family. Fernando, it turned out, was an "illegal."

Fernando's story was not an exception in La Villita, but rather the norm. I had known that the majority of the neighborhood's residents were first-generation Mexican immigrants, but I had no idea that so many of them had entered our country illegally.

In 1986 President Reagan signed his controversial immigration-amnesty bill into law, opening a path to legal status for nearly three million undocumented immigrants. While that monumental law helped millions of people come out of the shadows of our society, it did little to fix the long-term problem. Our nation's incoherent immigration policy continued to ensure that it was just a matter of time before the population of illegal immigrants grew again.

Today we have close to eleven million undocumented immigrants in our nation – three and a

> You shall treat the stranger who sojourns with you as the native among you, and you shall love him as yourself, for you were strangers in the land of Egypt.
>
> Leviticus 19:34

half times the number in President Reagan's day. Many of them worship in our churches as our brothers and sisters in Christ.

When I moved to La Villita thirty-five years ago, I never intended to get involved in a contentious issue like immigration reform. My motivation was simply to reach my neighbors with the good news of Jesus Christ and to mobilize them to create a healthy, flourishing place to live. Yet as time went on, I heard too many stories from church members about the hardships of living and working without papers. Without legal status, they were often taken advantage of by their employers and endured indignity and abuse. Families I knew were repeatedly being devastated by sudden deportations.

Determined to find a way to help, I connected a number of my undocumented friends with World Relief to get them immigration counseling. I was ready to pay whatever fees were necessary to get them the legal documentation they needed. I soon found how little I could do, thanks to a broken immigration system that made it virtually impossible for anyone coming into our country because of economic hardship to get legal status.

As time went on, I found it impossible to keep closing my eyes to this systematic inhumanity. I became convinced that in order to truly help my immigrant brothers and sisters caught in the web of this dysfunctional system, I needed to add an essential component to my ministry: the confrontation of injustice. Instead of simply blaming the undocumented for crossing our borders without legal permission, I had to recognize that the root causes are far deeper and broader than their risky

> Whatever you did for one of the least of these brothers and sisters of mine, you did for me.
>
> Matthew 25:40

decision to move north. Millions of men, women, and children were suffering terribly, and many of them were my neighbors.

Living side-by-side with my undocumented brothers and sisters, I saw that inviting them to one more Bible study, providing them with another bag of groceries, or establishing another program to bolster their education would not address a fundamental problem in their lives. Unexpectedly, I found myself working to change national immigration policy as an extension of my local ministry. As my CCDA colleague Mary Nelson remarked about our work in poor communities: "Instead of focusing on pulling drowning people out of the river, we need to go upstream to find out who is pushing them into the water in the first place!"

The more serious I became about addressing these systemic problems, the more convinced I became that it was not just the unlawful behavior of undocumented individuals that created the mess we were in. Large segments of our economy depended on the cheap labor provided by undocumented workers, who were now being scapegoated and blamed for problems with which they had nothing to do. In particular, the terrorist acts of 9/11 and the Great Recession beginning in 2008 both triggered a harsh backlash against undocumented immigrants. I often ask the Lord why I was so blessed to have been born just a few miles north of the border in Texas as a United States citizen.

As I began advocating for immigrants, I found myself reexamining my theology and my understanding of biblical justice. This is not a topic on which the Bible is silent. From beginning to end, scripture points us to a God who puts the margins of society at the center of his love and concern. I was already convinced that as Christians, we are called to love and serve the poor in their distress. But now I was learning to see them as victims of specific forms of oppression and injustice. It was not just individuals who needed to be confronted with their sin; unjust systems needed to be confronted and changed as well.

As I read the Bible with new eyes, I was struck by God's desire for every human being to experience his love and his justice. Already the first chapter of Genesis reminds us that those now derogated as "illegals" are our fellow human beings, created like us in the image of God. Both the Mosaic Law and the Old Testament prophets pointed to the stranger and sojourner as the one we must treat with justice and love. Oppression of any kind is an abomination in the eyes of God, and as a Christian I am responsible to confront it.

In the life of Christ, in particular, I found a compelling portrait of a God who absolutely loves and sides with the poor and the stranger in society. God did not incarnate himself among the religious and political elite, but on the periphery of Roman and Jewish existence. He was conceived in the womb of a young unmarried woman, Mary, a fact that likely created much commotion her home village. In a way familiar to many urban young people today, she and her fiancé had to endure the scandal. Once their son was born, they were forced to flee to a neighboring nation to escape persecution. Like most immigrants, they could not find adequate housing in their time of transition and crisis.

Even a casual reading of Jesus's ministry in the Gospels reveals a constant preoccupation with those pushed aside by the mainstream. The widow, the lame, the outsider, the poor, and the rejected are the focal points of his

Bringing his *raspado* stand with him, this man from Oaxaca, Mexico entered the United States illegally in order to earn a livelihood.

Photograph courtesy of Eneas De Troya

encounters. When you throw a party, he taught, do not invite those who will return the favor. Instead, invite the outsider, the stranger, the weak, the broken, and the scandalously sinful – all those normally excluded from the invitation list. When asked to explain how to live out the Torah's two greatest commandments – to love God and to love one's neighbor – Jesus tells the story of a man beaten and broken by the side of the road who is left to die by the religious folks, but who is shown love, kindness, and mercy by an outsider.

Jesus' death on the cross is perhaps God's most radical act of identification with the marginalized and humiliated. God allowed his only Son to be crucified alongside criminals so that everyone in the human race would understand that no one is beyond redemption or inclusion in his kingdom.

When Christian immigration advocates quote the Bible, then, it is not a matter of arbitrarily hijacking this or that particular verse to prove our point. We are proclaiming a truth rooted in the entire story of God's redeeming work, culminating on the cross. This indeed is good news to the poor and the immigrant.

After years of working on immigration reform with little support from my conservative evangelical brethren, in 2013 I began to see a dramatic shift. To the surprise of many secular observers, respected evangelical leaders began to see that the call to welcome the immigrant is not primarily a political issue, but rather a demand of the gospel. (Protestant mainline and Roman Catholic churches have long supported immigration reform.) Today the Evangelical Immigration Table represents one of the broadest coalitions of evangelicals to come together on a common issue. A dozen principal member organizations – including CCDA, which I lead – have made a commitment to continue working together until our nation reforms a system that hurts people and hurts our country. We've taken this message to the streets of our towns and cities where we encounter these families, and to the halls of Congress.

Sadly, we can mark few successes so far. Our nation's inability to pass legislation to fix a broken immigration system is the reason for the humanitarian crisis we're now facing at the Mexico-Texas border. Unprecedented numbers of children are being caught and detained as they attempt to enter the United States without their parents; it's expected that up to seventy thousand of these unaccompanied minors from Central America will be detained this year alone.

What heartens me is to see the response of thousands of churches and other people of goodwill. They are showing a willingness to get involved in helping care for these vulnerable children, many of whom have been traumatized during their journey by fatigue, hunger, and sexual abuse by the coyotes who smuggle them across Mexico. As we minister to these hungry and thirsty strangers arriving in our land, we have an opportunity to minister to Christ himself.

I pray – and I urge others to pray – that we will see a just and fair immigration policy passed into law. One day, I hope to tell my grandchildren the story of how thousands of Christ's followers worked together to change how our society treats its most vulnerable members. Whenever I see the images of Central American children arrested at the border, I tremble to think how our nation's response must look in Jesus' eyes. All the more, at the end of time I long to hear his words: "Whatever you did for one of the least of these brothers and sisters of mine, you did for me."

Marc Chagall, *The Bride and Groom of the Eiffel Tower.* Oil on linen (1938–1939), Musée National d'Art Moderne, Paris.

Marriage

Can We Have Justice Without It?

ROBERT P. GEORGE

Raised in West Virginia as the grandson of immigrant coal miners, Robert P. George is now McCormick Professor of Jurisprudence at Princeton University. All the same, his renown as a public intellectual doesn't stop him from picking up his banjo.

Plough: *Jesus teaches us to seek first the kingdom of God and his justice, his righteousness (Matt. 6:33). Today "justice" has become a buzzword in Christianity and beyond. What does Jesus' justice look like?*

Professor George: Jesus is heir to the great tradition of the prophets who cried out for justice. But by justice he does not mean something narrow – claiming my rights, or even defending other people's rights (although the defense of rights is part of justice considered comprehensively). Instead, justice according to Jesus means establishing the kind of interaction and cooperation with others in which we truly love as Jesus loved: we must will the good of the other for his or her own sake.

What are the problems with talking about justice merely in terms of rights?

In our modern, post-enlightenment discourse we sometimes reduce justice to a very individualistic concept of rights. This has caused some critics of what is called "rights talk" to reject the very idea of rights. Such critics claim that speaking of "rights" amounts to capitulating to the modern cult of the imperial self,

and thus encouraging selfishness, self-regard, and self-interest in a sense so narrow that it is incompatible with Christian faith.

But when Jesus and the prophets speak about justice, they are not speaking of a narrowly individualistic rights-based conception of justice. Certainly we must honor the rights of all persons, but we must do far more than that. We must seek to establish a community in which all members can flourish. The goal is the flourishing of each human person in all the diverse aspects of his or her personality and being, including the social, moral, and spiritual.

So when we think of justice in Christian terms, we need to make sure we understand justice in far richer ways than it is typically conceived in contemporary political or academic discourse.

You mentioned the prophets. Let's look at justice through the eyes of prophets like Amos, Isaiah, and Jeremiah, who kept hammering away at a few core themes: idolatry, the oppression of the worker, care of the widow and the orphan. What can we learn from them?

Idolatry is always a temptation; it is not something that Judaism wiped out or that

Christianity has cured. We will always be tempted to put something else in the place of God, and then (in effect) to worship it. That need not mean bowing down before a golden calf or a painted totem pole, which nowadays we can avoid easily enough. But do we worship money? Do we worship power, comfort, status, prestige? All of these things, which are not bad in themselves, become soul-imperiling when they are put in the place of God.

No matter how good the goal is – fighting poverty, protecting the environment, even defending people's fundamental human rights – if approached in the wrong way it can become idolatry. We have to worry not only about the temptation to do bad things, but also the temptation to do good things for bad reasons or in bad ways. A bad way is one that is not in line with the will of God and the dignity of human persons as creatures made in the divine image and likeness.

Jesus made a remarkable observation about the prophets in speaking of his cousin John the Baptist. He asked his listeners: "When you went out into the desert to see John the Baptist, who did you go to see? A prophet?" Then he told them: "I tell you, he is a prophet and more than a prophet" (Matt. 11:7–9). Here's the point: John was not a political figure; he was not someone working to establish a more just regime of economic or political relations. Instead, he called everyone to repentance: to turn away from sin and to turn back to God. What's more, he had a very concrete understanding of what sin is. We know this from the circumstances of his martyrdom. John, whom Jesus singles out as the greatest of all prophets, was killed because he railed against the illicit marriage of Herod. He protested the corruption of the institution of marriage by a political leader whose job was to serve the common good.

It would have been very easy and very safe for this great "prophet and more than a prophet" to keep his mouth shut about the king's private life. Yet John would not censor himself on the subject of sin. Because he understood the importance of the institution of marriage to the flourishing of human beings, and thus to the common good and to the very concept of justice, he fearlessly spoke out. His witness cost him his life.

Why Marriage Matters

You are one of the leading defenders of the traditional understanding of marriage as the union of one man and one woman for life. Why does marriage matter to the pursuit of justice?

If social justice is ultimately about the integral flourishing of human beings in society, then what could be more fundamental to justice than marriage? Marriage is the original and best department of health, education, and welfare. It plays an indispensable role in providing children with the structure, nurturing, and education that enables them both to flourish and to contribute to the flourishing of others. It enables them to become people who will respect themselves and respect others, and will order their own lives according to virtues like honesty, integrity, conscientiousness, the willingness to work hard, to defer gratification, and to respect the property and lives of others.

All these virtues are indispensable in any society, since its legal, political, and economic institutions depend on them. But these virtues aren't produced by legal, political, or economic institutions: they are produced by the family, which in turn is based on the marital covenant between husband and wife. When that is compromised – when the marriage culture begins to erode and then collapse in a community – the consequences are easy to see.

In this late season of our time on this planet, we have had enough experience with family breakdown, failure of family formation, sexual anarchy, and out-of-wedlock childbearing to know who the victims are. The victims are children – children who in such circumstances are often doomed to a life of delinquency, despair, drug abuse, criminality, violence, and incarceration in a vicious cycle. It's for their sake that we care about marriage as a public good.

I'm sometimes asked by colleagues: Even if you are right about marriage, why do you spend so much of your time on a "moral issue," as they put it? Why don't you concentrate on a real issue of social justice, such as fighting poverty? And I say to my friends: You really don't get it! Marriage is the greatest anti-poverty program that was ever created. In fact, it is so effective at enabling people to live in dignity and avoiding the collapse into poverty that one would almost be tempted to think that it is no mere human creation.

Are you saying that restoring the marriage culture will solve all social ills?

No, it's not going to be a panacea. It has got to be a part – a critical, even central part – of a larger effort at social reconstruction. People need jobs. Getting married is great, rebuilding the marriage culture is great, but fathers in particular need to have jobs. In so many cases today, men in impoverished areas cannot find work. So there is an important economic component to the problem as well. We must not fail to recognize that. But once you get the thing going properly, you will find there is a virtuous cycle: by rebuilding the marriage culture, you improve the culture of education, and thus people become more employable, which attracts employers to a community. Everything needs to be working together in the same direction. It works the opposite way too, of course: when marriage breaks down, the virtuous cycle turns into a vicious one. So we really do need to spare no effort in rebuilding the marriage culture.

Preach What You Practice
There are people who may agree with you, yet still object that absent a miracle, it may be too late to save the institution of marriage. How do you respond?

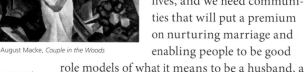

August Macke, *Couple in the Woods*

First of all, I believe in miracles. So our first obligation, I think, is to pray. We know there are real victims of the collapse of the marriage culture. For the sake of those victims we should be on our knees before God, asking for his blessing, never supposing that he is unable to help, while offering ourselves to be his instruments in rebuilding a vibrant marriage culture. The collapse was swift, and it's always a lot easier to tear down than to build up. I still believe it is not inevitable (as some say it is) that the next three to six generations will grow up without a healthy culture of marriage. With God's help, we can rebuild it.

Second, we need to model strong marriages in our own lives, and we need communities that will put a premium on nurturing marriage and enabling people to be good role models of what it means to be a husband, a wife, a father, a mother.

Third, we need to not only practice what we preach – we also need to preach.

That's not advice that Christians often hear.

Preaching is not popular. People say, "I don't want to sound preachy or condemn other people; I don't want to impose my values on others." Well, the prophets did not worry too much about that. When they saw that justice was in the balance they were willing to say what was on their minds.

We need to do the same. We need to go forth making the argument that marriage is the institution that brings together man and woman as husband and wife to be father and mother to any children born of their union, conferring on those children the inestimable blessing of being brought up in the loving, committed, covenantal bond of the mother and father whose union gave them life.

Portrait of a Roman couple from Herculaneum, ca. AD 79

The Chief End of Marriage

MUSONIUS RUFUS

The Stoic philosopher Gaius Musonius Rufus (ca. AD 100) lived in Rome as a contemporary of Nero, who banished him from the city because of his teaching. His lecture "On the Chief End of Marriage" is a remarkable statement by a thinker who stands outside the Judeo-Christian tradition.

Husband and wife should come together for the purpose of making a life in common and of bearing children, and furthermore of regarding all things in common between them, and nothing peculiar or private to one or the other, not even their own bodies. The birth of a human being which results from such a union is to be sure something marvelous, but it is not yet enough for the relation of husband and wife, inasmuch as quite apart from marriage it could result from other sexual unions, just as in the case of animals.

But in marriage there must be above all perfect companionship and mutual love of husband and wife, both in health and in sickness and under all conditions, since it was with desire for this as well as for having children that both entered upon marriage. Where, then, this love for each other is perfect and the two share it completely, each striving to outdo the other in devotion, the marriage is ideal and worthy of envy, for such a union is beautiful.

From Lecture XIIIa, in *Musonius Rufus,* vol. 10 of *Yale Classical Studies,* ed. Cora E. Lutz (Yale University Press, 1947).

Paying the Price

You made those arguments in your 2012 book What Is Marriage?. *In the two years since you and your co-authors wrote it, the very things your book sought to defend have taken a beating: the US Supreme Court struck down the Defense of Marriage Act, numerous states have redefined marriage to include same-sex relationships, and we've witnessed a procession of church leaders "evolving on marriage," just as President Obama has. Are you discouraged?*

As a West Virginia–born banjo player, I am a great lover of the traditional music of the mountains. One of my favorite songs comes from the Carter Family, who were among the first bands to record mountain music back in the 1920s and '30s. It's a hymn called "Hold Fast to the Right," and the chorus summarizes my messages to all Christians and all men and women of goodwill:

> Hold fast to the right, hold fast to the right,
> Wherever your footsteps may roam.
> Forsake not the way of salvation, my boy,
> That you learned from your mother at home.

We must hold fast to the right, however much others might "evolve." Marriage is a natural reality, testified to not only by the Bible in Genesis 2, but also by many great philosophical thinkers outside the Christian tradition: Plato, Aristotle, Xenophanes, Musonius Rufus, and Plutarch, all the way up through modern figures like Gandhi. We don't need to reinvent marriage; what we need to do is hold fast to the right.

Now, the problem is, of course, there are countless temptations today to deviate from the truth or to give up. You will be subjected to intimidation, your career might be jeopardized, your social standing in the community might be placed in peril, you may lose opportunities for honors and recognitions. We live at a time when witnessing to the truth about marriage comes at a price, though to be sure, not the price John the Baptist paid. Still, to lose a friend, to experience family discord, or to be branded as a bigot or homophobe is no fun.

You've been no stranger to such painful experiences. Who do you take inspiration from?

Well, certainly from Pope Francis. Recently I had the opportunity to meet Pastor Arnold of the Bruderhof communities after having read his wonderful book *Sex, God, and Marriage*. No one can be in the presence of such a man without being inspired; he is one of my new heroes. And I see wonderful young people out there who are doing bold and brilliant work, for instance my young co-authors Sherif Girgis and Ryan Anderson, and other former students such as Melissa Moschella and Micah Watson. In the Southern Baptist community, there's Russell Moore, and in the Jewish community I take great inspiration from Rabbi Meir Soloveichik, who is another of my former students. And of course, there are great intellectual heroes such as Mary Ann Glendon, Hadley Arkes, Leon Kass, Gilbert Meilaender, and rabbis David Novak and Jonathan Sacks. I could go on, but I have been blessed with so many role models and heroes old and young, Protestant and Catholic, Christian and Jewish. I am one blessed guy.

On Truth and Humility
You have surprised people by your friendship with Cornel West, the famous Afro American Studies scholar and talk-show host who often takes positions radically opposed to yours, including on marriage, affirmative action, criminal justice, foreign policy in the Middle East, and a host of other hotly contested issues.

There is no bond between two people more powerful, in my opinion, than a shared love of truth. That will include the desire to be corrected when one is in error. My vocation as a scholar and as a Christian is to get at the truth. That means I need to avoid falling so deeply in love with my own opinions that I prefer holding them, even when they are erroneous,

to being corrected. Cornel West sees his vocation in exactly the same way. I love my dear brother Cornel because he is a lover of truth. Yes, we have important differences of opinion, but they are relativized because of this shared love of the truth. Ours is really a cooperative venture in pursuit of a common good: "West and George, Partners. Business: Truth-Seeking." So when we engage each other, we know that neither of us is seeking victory – something only one party in a contest can acquire. Rather, both of us are seeking truth – a *common* good that interlocutors can share.

Christians have a special kind of relationship to the truth, because Jesus told us, "I am the way, the truth, and the life." No matter what domain we seek truth in, at the end of the day we are seeking Christ. That is why we should always be open to fraternal correction.

Openness to being corrected isn't a habit that's often associated with the fight over marriage.

It is tough to be both passionate for justice and righteousness, yet also detached enough to be willing to entertain criticism, knowing it's just possible that one might be wrong. But we have to do that; we need to keep an open mind.

I have made something of a career out of criticizing the thought of the great nineteenth-century liberal thinker John Stuart Mill, especially his 1859 essay *On Liberty*. Yet right in the middle of that essay, in the chapter "Of the Liberty of Thought and Discussion," Mill makes a compelling point. He shows, in effect, that all of us need to earn the right to have our opinions, and we do that by considering very carefully, sympathetically, and in the best possible light what reasonable people who disagree with us have to say.

Now when I say "earn the right to an opinion," I certainly do not mean earn the right to freedom from government interference with the expression of one's views. What I do mean is that if you don't understand why some reasonable people of goodwill disagree with you, then you don't really grasp the basis of your own view, you don't have a grip on *the reasons* for holding it. You are a mere ideologue. That's why the kind of open-mindedness Mill calls for – in other words, the virtue of intellectual humility – is critically important.

Renewing the Church

Christian teaching on marriage and sexuality has never been so much at odds with the wider culture since the first few centuries of Christianity, when Christians were a minority in the pagan Roman Empire. In what ways can the early church serve as a model to us?

Here I face a particular challenge, and I am in no position to preach to others. The model of the early church is one of living with simplicity not for the sake of simplicity itself, but for the sake of the gospel, so that no worldly things impede one's devotion to Christ. And that is something I find very hard. I am not good at it. Yet that is the model the early church gives us. I have enormous admiration for those who seek to live in this way, whether within monastic communities or communities such as the Bruderhof, or simply as lay people striving to live simply.

Your effort in the Bruderhof community to live the gospel on the model of the early Christians is certainly great for your own growth in faith, but I hope you understand that it is not simply for your own spiritual benefit. It is for all of us, even those of us who lead very different lives. We receive an enormous benefit from your example of discipleship, simplicity, and generosity, and from your willingness to live out both the teachings of the Ten Commandments and the virtues of the Sermon on the Mount. Even more importantly, we on the outside benefit from your prayers. I encourage you with all my heart to remain faithful to this vocation. I repeat, it's not for your own benefit, but for the sake of other Christians and the whole world.

In the Catholic Church, we now have Pope Francis who models his own personal life on the example of the Christians in the early church, carrying his own bags, living in humble abodes, avoiding the grand trappings of the monarchical papacy. He is a great example not only for those of us who are Catholic but really for all Christians and for all people.

Why have Christians been so ineffectual in offering a living alternative to the materialistic and hedonistic culture around us? How does the church need to change?

The church should not be soft-spirited, any more than we should imagine that God is soft-spirited. The church should be willing to speak truth, including to her own people. How many clergy do not want to offend their congregants, and so pass over in silence many of the moral demands of the Christian faith! They fail to speak up to defend the lives of innocent unborn children or the institution of marriage. They fear that people will be offended by a priest or minister preaching the whole gospel.

If we are going to speak truth to power, which we need to do, let's start by speaking truth to our own Christian people. Clergy need to speak truth to their congregations, and all church members need to speak truth to one another.

"Well no," people may say, "I don't want to bring up controversial issues; it will bring division in the church." They'll even misuse the Sermon on the Mount: "Blessed are the peacemakers. . . ." Or they will misappropriate, "Judge not lest you be judged." But here we must remember another word of Jesus: "I did not come to bring peace but the sword." Sometimes division is the price that must be paid for speaking the truth. Let's recall again the man whom Jesus praised above all others: John the Baptist. Do you think John the Baptist worried for even three seconds that he was being divisive in his preaching? We need to follow his example. ⤳

Interview by Peter Mommsen on June 25, 2014.
Watch the video version at www.plough.com.

Egon Schiele, *House with Drying Laundry*

Living Justly
One Disconnect at a Time

CHARLES E. MOORE

W hen I heard the call of Christ at seventeen, I thought all that mattered was eternal salvation and my personal relationship with Jesus. I only needed to read my Bible, pray, and keep my life free of sin.

But my Bible reading soon got me into trouble when I realized that Jesus didn't just want a personal relationship with me; he wanted everything. "Seek first the kingdom of God," Jesus taught, "and his righteousness." He called for more than spiritual fulfillment. This everything for the sake of God's kingdom would completely derail my own plans and aspirations.

During college I read Ronald Sider's book *Rich Christians in an Age of Hunger.* I shouldn't have had to read it to learn about poverty – I'd grown up vaguely aware of the stark contrast between the upper-middle-class neighborhood where I lived and Oakland, just twenty miles west, with its squalor, crime, and ravaged neighborhoods. But the reason for such disparity had never occurred to me; I assumed that the world would continually get better until such conditions were eliminated.

The author, *left,* with a homeless neighbor, Denver

Now Sider's book destroyed that cozy mindset. It exposed how disconnected my faith was from the world that God intended – and how disconnected I was from the rest of humanity. My indifferent, success-driven outlook was in many ways responsible for others' suffering. Sider's plea to rich Christians like me was to submit to God's plan for his people. This would mean a drastic change in my life, one for which I wasn't ready.

But God was ready. Once he had pried open my eyes wide enough to see the gulf between the haves and have-nots, the Bible then smashed my remaining rationalizations to bits. Jesus' words in Luke 4 caught hold of me – he proclaimed good news to the poor, freedom for prisoners, sight for the blind, release to the oppressed, and a social revolution to inaugurate God's jubilee. The Old Testament's vision of justice and peace, where every person could live with dignity, safe from greedy landlords and enterprising profiteers, helped transform my Christian imagination. Jesus, the fulfillment of God's promise, brought salvation from all sin – from structures of oppression as well as from evil desires.

In the church I attended, I heard precious little of this message. Most of my Christian friends went through life like everybody else – the church simply baptized our culture's rituals of spending and consuming. A chasm gaped between the individualistic Christianity I knew and the new world the Bible had opened up to me.

By the time I left seminary, my quest to live according to God's justice had thrown me into spiritual turmoil. Etched inside me was the biblical vision of justice, yet around me I saw a world of unbelievable suffering and injustice. I was then reading Bonhoeffer, Yoder, Gutierrez, Tolstoy, Wolterstorff, and Moltmann, who each in their way made me feel even more keenly the sharp edge of Jesus' teachings, such as his command to lay up treasures in heaven rather than on earth.

One day I couldn't stand it anymore. I took everything I owned – barring a few clothes, books, and my 1964 VW Bug – and deposited it at a local Salvation Army store. Now I went on a campaign to "live simply so that others can simply live." I bought only used items, ate two meals a day instead of three, and marched on behalf of social causes. I stopped paying a portion of federal income tax to protest war, sending the money to humanitarian projects in poor countries instead. Wishing to live in solidarity with the city's homeless, I moved to inner-city Denver. Echoing in my heart and mind were the prophet Micah's words: "What does the Lord require of you but to do justice, to love mercy, and to walk humbly with your God?" (Micah 6:8)

But what did this look like in practice? For several years I sought the answer in ever more radical changes to my lifestyle. Meanwhile my activist friends, well-intentioned and dedicated, were either burning out, conflating their faith with liberal politics, or turning their social concerns, as it seemed to me, into hobbies that enabled them to live much like everyone else – a "conscious" variety of consumerism with an extra dash of self-righteousness.

While working on my doctorate, I zealously taught seminary students to re-read their Bibles focusing on God's concern for the poor. By this time I was married, and my wife Leslie and I were living with others in a shared household, reducing our expenses still further. We sponsored a child in South America, volunteered at a homeless ministry, and helped a friend start a food pantry in the warehouse district.

But I soon began to realize how little such efforts could fix. The cycle of poverty, the breakdown of the family, drug abuse, sexual exploitation, militarism, urban decay, suicide, and domestic violence were all symptoms of a deeper malaise, one rooted in a sick and sinful worldview in which I myself was still deeply invested.

It began to dawn on me that I was part of the problem. While seeking to pursue a just world, I had continued to drink from the fountain of privilege, laying plans to secure my own livelihood in a vocation agreeable to me, choosing my own lifestyle, pursuing my own dreams. How did any of this make for true justice, in which everyone's needs are met, everyone's dignity is respected, and all are their brother's and sister's keeper? How could a self-sufficient, private life based on private property possibly be in harmony with the biblical vision of sacrifice, sharing, solidarity, and service? How could I work for justice on behalf of the downtrodden when so much of my time was spent taking care of myself?

My friends kept telling me to cool it. I was too hard on myself, they said, and my radicalism was unrealistic and theologically ungrounded. Between the "now" and the "not yet" of God's kingdom, I had to find a compromise: spiritual vitality, yes, the kingdom of God's justice, no; personal integrity, yes, but a new social order, no. Our task as Christians was to love God, love one another, and with any surplus, help those we can.

But didn't Christ want us to give not just our surplus, but rather everything, like the widow with her two copper coins? And what about Micah's vision – did living between the

Is not this the fast that I choose:
    to loose the bonds of injustice,
    to undo the thongs of the yoke,
to let the oppressed go free,
    and to break every yoke?
Is it not to share your bread with the hungry,
    and bring the homeless poor into your house;
when you see the naked, to cover them,
    and not to hide yourself from your own kin?
Then your light shall break forth like the dawn,
    and your healing shall spring up quickly;
your vindicator shall go before you,
    the glory of the Lord shall be your rear guard.
Then you shall call, and the Lord will answer;
    you shall cry for help, and he will say, Here I am.
If you remove the yoke from among you,
    the pointing of the finger, the speaking of evil,
if you offer your food to the hungry
    and satisfy the needs of the afflicted,
then your light shall rise in the darkness
    and your gloom be like the noonday.

Isaiah 58:6–10

"now" and the "not yet" mean that we couldn't live justly, love mercy, and walk humbly?

Meanwhile, our work with the poor brought disappointments. Billy, a homeless man who got by with a bit of cash from washing windows, didn't want to leave the streets. Even after we had helped him get an apartment, he liked it better under bridges – he didn't have to pay rent, he argued. Gale was another such case, a middle-aged woman living in subsidized housing who was repeatedly evicted because her apartment was filled with cat feces. She wanted her cats, and that was that.

At first these experiences, and many others like them, stumped me. Still, I wondered how different I really was from Billy and Gale. Was I willing to give up running my own life on my own terms?

Rubbernecking

The art of the century is to hear
sun through mulberry,
small ball of white light centered
in torn leaves. We are not
biblical? Here in grounded
in verse as children while
the poor present alms to the poor,
we are freedom finding itself.

We have no answers.
Some of us missed the broadcast
to success. The neighborhood
fills with unseen deep-throated
robins. Remember
what it means to be alone
we say, disliking or loving
mad streets, where the broken
fearlessly ride buses.
We cannot fix the contest
outside, even if we
rubberneck our way
through accident and luck.

SHERYL LUNA

It was at this point I had to rethink my faith from the ground up, especially my understanding of the church. In my efforts to live justly, I had almost forgotten about the church and the role she plays in God's economy. To be sure, by now several of us were part of a fellowship where white folk in the hood and friends from the burbs could worship together with the poor on the streets. That was wonderful – except that something was terribly missing. When the service ended, we all returned to our separate worlds, as if our Sunday morning community didn't exist. Our avant-garde fellowship still consisted of an "us" and "them." It was a far cry from the common life of the first church in Jerusalem, where all who belonged to Christ were as one family.

After all, the earliest Christians gave witness to a new social order and a spirituality that encompassed every facet of life. Among them, conversion to Christ expressed itself in a life where everything was shared in common, nobody was in need or forgotten, and racial, gender, and social divisions were overcome. Wasn't this the new creation in Christ that Paul spoke of: a new way of being human, beyond self-interest, based on repentance and self-sacrifice (2 Cor. 5:17)?

Now when I opened the Bible, I saw that God wanted a people, distinct from the nations, who lived an altogether different kind of life together, one made possible by his Spirit. In the church the economics of *koinonia,* in which love and justice are united, could become a reality – one available to all those willing to surrender their independence to become part of a practical life of unity. Among this people, the inner and the outer, the personal and the social realms of existence could join in harmony.

I came to realize that justice does not consist of heroic good works by the well-off few or a set of new policies imposed by the enlightened on the many. It grows from the bottom up and from the inside out, through forging a life with others willing to take up the cross and voluntarily let go of their own pursuits. To fight for justice, then, I needed to change. I had to live in such a way that the very systems that fostered disenfranchisement and the ideologies that kept people apart were rendered obsolete. Wasn't this what the church is for – to be the "new humanity" in Christ? "Turn around! The kingdom of God is at hand! Behold, I make all things new!"

Eventually my wife and I were compelled to leave everything behind – career, home, family, ministry, possessions – and threw our lot in with the Bruderhof, a group of folks who sought to live together in such a way that justice is a daily, concrete reality available to all, rich and poor.

This certainly hasn't proved to be the end of the journey. I'm still living in relative privilege in a world where millions suffer want – a world of child hunger, mass incarceration, and organized exploitation. The distance between my professed faith and actual practice hasn't magically vanished.

Yet the community in which my wife and I share, imperfect as it inevitably remains, is a gift of God's Spirit – the same Spirit who spoke through Micah, who gathered the first church at Pentecost, and who will one day be "poured out on all flesh" (Acts 2:14–21). My prayer is that more people will join us on this journey. Surely the world needs the good news of God's reign of justice – and it needs a people who demonstrate this justice as a tangible reality through the life of peace that they share. ⤳

Charles E. Moore is co-editor of the Blumhardt Series from Plough Publishing and Cascade Books, which includes most recently the C.F. Blumhardt volume The Gospel of God's Reign: Living for the Kingdom of God *(2013).*

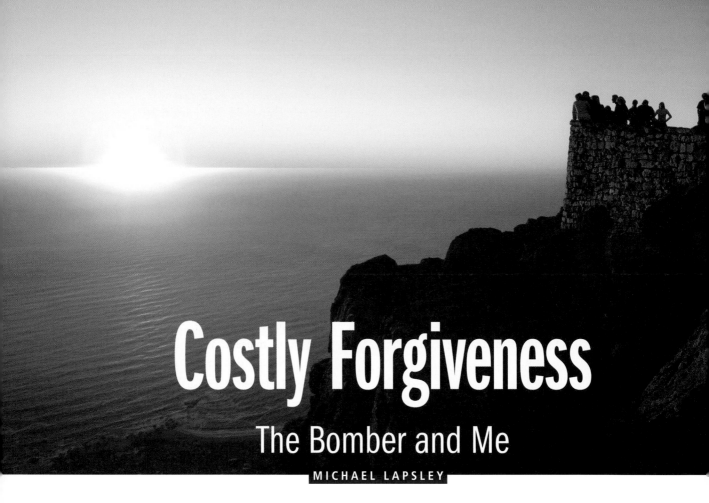

Costly Forgiveness

The Bomber and Me

MICHAEL LAPSLEY

A crowd awaits sunset on Table Mountain, Cape Town, South Africa

In April 1990, three months after Nelson Mandela was released from prison, I was living in Zimbabwe working for Mandela's African National Congress movement. One day I received by mail an envelope with two religious magazines. When I opened it, the package exploded, destroying both my hands and one eye, shattering my eardrums, and inflicting many other injuries.

To this day I can clearly recall how when the bomb went off I had the distinct sense that God was with me. I felt that the great promise of scripture had been kept: "Lo I am with you always, even to the end of the age" (Matt. 28:20).

Now whenever I tell my story, I am not bitter, and I don't want revenge. But forgiveness? In reality, I haven't forgiven anybody, because there's still no one to forgive – I don't know who made the bomb, who wrote my name on the envelope, who sent it. Sometimes I speculate about what it would be like to meet those responsible. Perhaps one day there will be a

---

Father Michael Lapsley, a member of the Anglican Society of the Sacred Mission, has worked in South Africa since 1973. As a student chaplain during the 1976 Soweto Uprising, he protested atrocities committed against schoolchildren by the apartheid government and was expelled from the country as a result. Today he is director of the Institute for Healing of Memories in Cape Town, South Africa, and the author of Redeeming the Past: My Journey from Freedom Fighter to Healer *(Orbis, 2012).*

knock on the door, and a person will be standing there saying: "I am the one who sent you that letter bomb, will you forgive me?" How will I respond? I might say, "Excuse me, sir, do you still make letter bombs?" "No," he might reply, "now I work at the local hospital. Will you forgive me?" Then I would answer, "Yes, I forgive you, and I would prefer that you spend the next fifty years working in the hospital instead of being locked up."

I believe one thousand times more in the justice of restoration than the justice of punishment. So often when we say "justice," we mean punishment or even revenge, but of course there is another kind of justice: the justice of restoring relationships. Perhaps I would drink tea with the letter-bomber and tell him, "Well sir, I have forgiven you, but I still have no hands, only one eye, and my eardrums are damaged. I'll always need someone to assist me for the rest of my life. Of course you will help pay for that person, not as a condition of forgiveness, but as part of your effort to make reparation and restitution."

In the Christian community especially, we often speak of forgiveness in a way that's glib and cheap and easy. My experience, however, is that for most human beings, forgiveness is costly, painful, and difficult. And yet, when it happens, there is mutual liberation. The Greek word the New Testament uses for forgiveness also means "untying a knot."

Pain connects people. Much of my work is in South Africa's black community, and my passport to that community is the fact that I have suffered. When I was working in the Trauma Centre for Victims of Violence and Torture in Capetown, an African woman once came to see me and began to tell her story. I offered to refer her to one of our psychiatrists. "No," she said, "I've already seen them. I want to talk to you." I asked her why. "Because you know suffering and pain."

In this way, the loss of my hands and eye, which is dramatic and visible, becomes a passport to other people's brokenness, which often is not visible but is no less real. Brokenness is the norm for the human family; perfection is not. Those of us with conspicuous physical disabilities remind the rest of the human family of the truth about all of us.

One characteristic of our age is the phenomenon of unfinished business coming back to bite societies that have sought to bury their past rather than to heal it. When apartheid ended in South Africa, we faced two giant questions: How can we get people water, electricity, education, and healthcare? And how do we deal with what we have done to each other? In any place of conflict, the transition towards justice must deal with psychological, emotional, and spiritual issues as well as politics and economics.

Even when there is a just settlement of a conflict, if people are full of hatred, bitterness, and desire for revenge, it will never create a good society. Leaders must come to terms with this. If Nelson Mandela, when he walked out of prison after twenty-seven years, would have said, "Now it's time to get them," we would have died by the millions. But what did he say? "Never again shall it be that this beautiful land will again experience the oppression of one by another." ⤳

Based on an interview by Richard Mommsen on May 7, 2014. Read or watch the rest of the interview at www.plough.com.

Heroes
Now It's Your Turn

MAXIMILIAN PROBST

I have a storytelling problem. One late summer afternoon – it must have been in the 1990s, I was still in high school – I sat on the riverbank looking out at the water. With me were a friend of mine and the girl of my dreams. She told a story, I forget it now, but I remember her next words: "Now you guys tell a story. Just anything, whatever comes to mind."

My throat clamps shut. I hear my friend good-naturedly stringing words together, knowing I'm next. The moment comes, and I can't even mouth one syllable. The sight of the river lying heavy in front of me, yellowish brown under the perpetually gray sky, the Elbe River in Hamburg.

Why don't I just say something, anything? Why is it that to this day, whenever I'm asked to tell a story I go blank?

My father also never told stories. Perhaps that's because his own father *was* a story, one that is in the history books: a story we remember with pride and in silence, day in day out, a story that is unspeakably painful, in my father's case of course far more so even than in mine.

Once in high school a teacher asked me to tell my grandfather's story. I got as far as two or three sentences, and then I couldn't stop crying.

No, stories and I don't get along. But here's the thing: nowadays if you can't tell stories, you're a loser.

Modern advertising clips don't show us products – they tell us narratives about people and smartphones, people and cars, people and beer brands.

Campaign strategists work to position politicians so that a story takes hold in the heads of the voters – for instance, the story of the cool-headed expert who saves the country with his superior knowledge.

Maximilian Probst, born in 1977, is a German journalist.

Senior citizens pay professional biographers handsomely to record their life experiences, recasting the commonplace as a saga. And younger people write the chronicle of their lives in Facebook posts, chronicles that grow vaster and more boundless with every passing day.

Stories, stories everywhere, capturing revenue, securing power, conferring status.

I'm a journalist, so storytelling should come easy. But something in me resists.

That's why I'm sitting here in this seminar room of Cologne's RTL School of Journalism together with six women and two men, staring at a flat screen that flickers with the slogan: STORIES MEAN SUCCESS. In front sits Uwe Walter, age forty-eight, stocky, cheerful eyes, a nose that's anything but bashful, chest out, his whole person seeming to be one single motion forward. Walter is a consultant for practically all the radio and television broadcasters in Germany as well as for many scriptwriters, newspaper editors, advertising agencies, and public-relations firms. He calls himself a "storytelling coach."

Walter believes that he's found the recipe for a good story. He's willing to let us in on it.

As we set out on our quest for what makes a good story, Walter says, we could start with the Bible, with its exciting stories about Noah, Solomon, and Moses. Or we could start with the story of the Babylonian king Gilgamesh, or with the equally ancient story from India of Arjuna, who fights a heroic battle against an enemy clan.

These centuries-old myths, says Walter, were written down at different times and in different cultures and places. Yet amazingly, their narrative structure is similar. Each revolves around a main character that changes and develops through facing defeats and disappointments. At the end, this main character is transformed into what had been dormant within him all along: a hero.

Buddha, Noah, Moses, Gilgamesh, Arjuna, Jesus of Nazareth: human beings clearly are drawn by a certain kind of story, Walter says. The reason why these narratives took shape in precisely this form and became so influential is that they meet a core human need.

The room becomes quiet, and Uwe Walter tells us about a man who claimed to have deciphered the DNA of myths – all myths. He was an American called Joseph Campbell, whose book *The Hero with a Thousand Faces* was published in 1949. According to Campbell, there is a pattern that all hero narratives (approximately) follow: the hero receives a call to adventure, departs, meets a mentor, finds comrades, undergoes trials, fights a decisive battle, and then returns, having gained an appropriate reward. Thus, says Campbell, Buddha finds enlightenment, Jesus sits at the right hand of God, and Gilgamesh learns that only great deeds will guarantee him immortality. In all cases, the hero's journey remains fundamentally the same.

Campbell's model is so simple it's contagious. It can help us not only to understand old stories, but also to create new ones – stories that infiltrate people's brains and stay there, regardless of whether it's the story of a new Mercedes model, or the story of the first black presidential candidate.

Campbell's book is still selling well in Hollywood today.

Star Wars, Harry Potter, and *Lord of the Rings* – all hero journeys, all stories that describe a transformation. They fascinate us because in actuality each of us wants to be changed, to venture forth from our tired daily grind. Everyone wants to be a hero. According to Walter.

And now it's our turn. Marlys, Ariana, Yanina, Martina, Lisa, Philip, Catherine, Daniel – and me.

Uwe Walter asks us to introduce ourselves, not with dry biographical facts but with anecdotes that apply what we've learned. His special challenge to us: we shouldn't shy away from mentioning problems, if we're OK with that, even including – if only symbolically – death, which after all makes the best stories.

We take a dive into nine lives.

As they tell, my fellow participants are relaxed and self-confident. Apparently they have thought of a topic immediately. The fact that their stories are highly personal doesn't seem to bother them.

Marlys, a media researcher, tells about her divorced and frequently remarried parents, and how she herself married her childhood boyfriend – but only after she had first located a wedding venue where her estranged parents could all celebrate without having to cross paths.

Ariana, a public-relations executive for a firm stuck in negative headlines, tells how she took the stage to speak at an industry event – and the whole audience erupted in catcalls and boos.

Yanina, also in public relations, tells how for two years she got up at 4:30 every morning to work on her novel – and how she suffered a collapse.

Lisa tells of growing up as the daughter of a preacher in a strict religious family and being awestruck by the lead actress in a hairspray commercial who disembarks from a Concorde perfectly coiffed – and how she herself became a society reporter.

Later Walter will tell us that all these stories are hero journeys. In each, two questions are always central: Will I find the right man or woman for me? And will I find the calling that fulfills me? In addition, he will say, another question lurks in the background: Do I run my life, or is it controlled by others? Do I make my own decisions, or do I just accept whatever comes my way?

I'm next. I don't say a word about my grandfather or his death. Instead, I recount how I'm embarrassed to still be living in Hamburg, since despite wanting to move to Rome with my wife and children I still haven't yet dared to do so, even though all I'd need to do is sign the house rental agreement that's lying at home on my desk. "Rome or death!" I say, quoting Italian freedom fighter Garibaldi.

The word "hero" seems ever more ridiculous.

What if heroes are actually a thing of the past? Do we live in a "post-heroic age"? That's the term used by sociologists and political scientists to describe societies like ours that combine affluence with low birth rates. Members of a post-heroic society, so the argument runs, have too much to lose, ensconced as they are in their prosperity. Rather than surrendering themselves to a great cause like heroes of old, they prefer to pursue their own well-being. Even Angelina Jolie, hailed not long ago as a hero for undergoing a mastectomy to prevent breast cancer, took radical action only as a means of saving herself.

No, we aren't surrounded by heroes today, but rather by a set narrative. We could call it "pop heroism" – heroism without a true hero, heroism conceived as a metaphor for self-actualization. Pop heroism teaches us to take whatever we can get – without reminding us that the true hero is always the one who gives. Hemingway still knew this when he wrote, "Winner take nothing." To be a true hero is a gift that often takes the form of a sacrifice. Historian Johan Huizinga defines heroism as "the heightened awareness of being personally called to participate in the realization of a task for the common good, dedicating all one's energies up to and including the sacrifice of oneself."

What is left of this definition when the word hero is applied, for example, to athletes competing for titles and trophies? Does the tennis star Sabine Lisicki participate in a task for the common good when she vies to dominate the turf in Wimbledon?

Doesn't this kind of "hero journey" really just hijack a noble word as a way of legitimizing ultimately trivial strivings for personal success? Isn't it a sweet poison that intoxicates us so that we forget the things that really matter?

Uwe Walter is convinced of the opposite. He believes in the healing power of hero stories. He believes that if we want to make the most of our humanity, then we should all live according to the recipe of Campbell's fundamental myth.

Why did Sabine Lisicki lose in Wimbledon? According to Campbell, the answer is: because she was not inwardly ready. Perhaps she is repressing something that still needs to be processed. But this defeat will, according to the doctrine of the hero journey, prove to be a necessary stage for Lisicki. From it she will learn to use her heroic potential fully and completely. And the day will come when she will triumph.

Campbell's gospel of salvation also offers good news to the participants in the seminar. Ariana, the PR executive who was booed off stage, will one day be honored for her company magazine; Yanina, the stymied author, will win the Bachmann Prize; and I will assuredly one day live in Rome.

With these happy prospects in view, we end the day of the seminar in a dignified, somewhat dimly lit restaurant overlooking the Rhine. Walter continues to bubble forth, his energy apparently inexhaustible.

It occurs to me that it's not by chance that the hero idea is so popular just now. In a Europe where social safety nets are being cut, one can always say to those being pushed into the void, "You are heroes, you'll make out fine."

The hero concept also has its cynical sides.

For if there really was equality of opportunity, if everyone really did have the ideal start in life, then we could freely affirm Joseph Campbell's claim that whosoever seeks will find doors that open unexpectedly. But here in our society? Isn't it rather true that Hollywood-style hero stories have the effect of kicking people who are down while delivering the spiteful sermon: you could have been heroes, but you aren't and it's all your fault.

In reality, the question that Walter never ceases to ask – "Do you make decisions, or do you simply accept what comes your way?" – ought to be asked not just individualistically, but collectively, as a movement. Then it would thunder through our hollowed-out democracy with a roar to make political and financial elites tremble. Do we make decisions? Or do we simply accept what is imposed on us, what is forced down our throats with the magic words "no alternative" and "objective necessity"? Could the rhetoric of the hero journey transform individualists into revolutionary actors?

Questions and more questions.

What does Walter say to all this? That I'm refusing to embark on my hero journey. That I won't take the leap. That I'm a wimp, a brooder, a scaredy-cat. That my manhood is suspect. That I'm just chicken.

This is meant as provocation, of course. Walter is trying everything to coax the hero out of me.

It's almost midnight and we leave the restaurant; Walter heads back to his room. I still haven't told my story. It's not mine anyway, but the story of my grandfather.

Photograph by George (Jürgen) Wittenstein / AKG-Images

What Was the White Rose?

In summer 1942, German university students Hans Scholl and Alexander Schmorell began secretly writing and distributing leaflets signed by "the White Rose," calling themselves Germany's "bad conscience." Although by this time the Nazis' crimes were widely known even in Germany, shamefully few people had the courage to protest. The members of the White Rose were among the few exceptions.

Scholl and Schmorell were eventually joined by others including their philosophy professor Kurt Huber, fellow students Christoph Probst and Willi Graf, and Hans Scholl's younger sister, Sophie. Through their underground publishing, they urged the German people to "support the Resistance" by resisting Nazi commands, sabotaging the war effort, and duplicating and distributing White Rose leaflets. The last leaflet, drafted by Christoph Probst and targeted at Munich's university students, concluded: "Our people stand ready to rebel against the Nationals Socialist enslavement of Europe in a fervent new breakthrough of freedom and honor."

Hans and Sophie Scholl were arrested on February 18, 1943; they, together with Christoph Probst, were tried and executed four days later. Kurt Huber and Alexander Schmorell followed them to the guillotine in July, and Willi Graf in October.

The White Rose members were prompted in their lonely and dangerous stand by common decency, but sustained in it by their profound faith. In the words of their fourth leaflet:

> Everywhere and at all times demons lurk in the dark, waiting for the moment when man is weak; when of his own volition he leaves his place in the order of creation as founded for him by God. . . . When he yields to the force of evil, he separates himself from the powers of a higher order; and after voluntarily taking the first step, he is driven on to the next and the next at a furiously accelerating rate. Man is free, to be sure, but without the true God he is defenseless against evil.

To find out more about the White Rose, see Inge Scholl's classic account The White Rose *(Wesleyan, 1970).*

Back in high school, I told the story as far as when, on February 18, 1943 in Hitler's Germany, Hans and Sophie Scholl scattered the last packets of their subversive leaflets in the atrium of Munich University. I never told how the janitor discovered them, locked the outside doors to the building, and arrested them. How Hans, as he was being arrested, started shredding a piece of paper. The Gestapo later reassembled the pieces, which proved to be the handwritten draft of a leaflet penned by my grandfather, Christoph Probst, to protest the Nazis and their crimes. A few days later he was arrested in Innsbruck, transported to Munich, and brought to trial in expedited proceedings together with Hans and Sophie. For the sake of his family he fought for his life, and Hans and Sophie did all they could to protect him. To no avail. Roland Freisler, the Nazi regime's highest judge for political crimes, convicted him together with the Scholls in a show trial and sentenced him to death. The sentence was carried out a few hours later. My grandfather was never able to say goodbye to his wife and his three small children. To his mother he managed to write: "Tell them that my death was easy and joyful."

For me, this has always been the only true story. As for other stories, including my own: what significance do they have in comparison? Practically none. That's why I object to using the word "hero" in an inflationary way. I'm unable to regard the rest of us, who supposedly are each somewhere on our hero journeys, as heroes. I cannot accept "heroes of the workplace" and "family heroes." Heroism starts when we leave the realm of the personal, and yes, when we leave the realm of family.

Let no one think that this kind of hero is obsolete in our post-heroic age. Even if parliamentary democracy seems to legitimate our wish to pursue only our private happiness – with the excuse that our public responsibility begins and ends with casting a ballot – even

Top left, members of the White Rose in June 1942: Hans Scholl (second from left), Raymund Samiller, Sophie Scholl and Alexander Schmorell.

so, let no one imagine that we live in the best of all possible worlds. Even in our post-heroic age, we're confronted on all sides by systematic injustice: injustice that cannot be bureaucratically legislated away, injustice that requires each of us to take responsibility and to act, contrary to our own comfort and our slowness of heart. So long as this remains so, heroism will continue to make its claim on us, regardless of time and place. Heroism will always start when people turn away from their own persons and place themselves in the service of a cause, a cause that may often only affect them indirectly, a cause in the service of others, of the disadvantaged, the persecuted, the oppressed, the tortured, the murdered.

At this point I can already hear post-heroic objections being raised: Can we please get this just a size smaller? If our standards of measurement are so gigantic, won't we relegate heroes to an exalted sphere where they are admired but not followed? Shouldn't we rather learn to see heroes merely as products of

their time, people no different from you and me?

As persuasive as that sounds, the exact opposite is true. The hankering to pull true heroes down from their pedestals seeks to comfort us with the false reassurance that we can remain as we are. Yet it's only through realizing how much heroes differ from us by virtue of their heroic deeds that we gain the ability to grow through their example. As the Scottish author Thomas Carlyle wrote: "Ah, does not every true man feel that he is himself made higher by doing reverence to what is really above him?"

No, hardly any of us are heroes, certainly not me. Everything I'm writing seems completely unrelated to my own life when compared with what my grandfather did.

But perhaps that doesn't matter. We need heroes, but not each of us needs to be one. The greatest gift that heroes offer us, I believe, is that we can remember them – and through remembering, take up our mundane and daily task of living an upright life. ✈

Below, Christoph Probst (1918– 1943) with his son Michael. Michael was three years old at the time of his father's death; his brother Vincent was two, his sister Katja was four weeks.

The Bell Ringer

A Story by Kwon Jeong-saeng

Translated by Won Maroo • Illustrated by Kang Woo-geun

It's early morning, four o'clock. The stars glitter across the dark sky. The roofs of the village sleep quietly, almost hidden by the persimmon grove. On a hill outside the village stands a little church with a little bell tower. The fresh morning winds race around the mountain ridge. Then quietly, quietly they gather around the church, as if dancing a gentle dance. They are waiting for the bell ringer to start ringing the bells, so that they can carry the sound of the chimes out into the world.

The bell ringer grasps the bell rope and, *soo-ook,* pulls it downward.

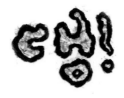

With a resounding clang, the first chime is born: *Deng!*

This first chime, I'll admit, is a mischief-maker and rascal. It flies down the hill to the little hut where Grandfather and Grandmother live, right on the outskirts of the village.

Grandfather is hard of hearing, so the first chime doesn't bother him at all. But Grandmother's ears are still as good as ever, and although she works hard all day, she's a light sleeper. Every morning when *Deng!* rings out, she wakes up with such a frightful start that her liver almost falls out.

Even so, Grandmother doesn't dislike this mischievous little chime. Not at all – in fact she always says, "A hundred thanks, a thousand thanks!" Then she gets up, wakes Grandfather, and goes with him to the church for morning prayer. And that's the way that the first chime, which rings out exactly at four o'clock, fulfills its duty of waking Grandmother in the little hut.

Now the bell ringer pulls down the rope again, lets it go, and watches it tumble upward. The second chime rings out: *Deng!*

The second chime tries to wake the miller who lives in his mill on the low rise near the stream. But the miller just makes a face, closes his eyes, and rolls over. Soon he is snoring again – he has always been a lazybones. Every day, the second chime's hopes are dashed: "I go to so much trouble to wake him, but he never gets up for morning prayer. What a good-for-nothing!"

While the second chime is trying to rouse the miller, the third and fourth chimes fly out, one to wake the woman in the date-palm house and the other to the cigarette-store man. Mrs. Kim, the woman in the date-palm house, is the church's deaconess. As soon as the third chime visits her, she turns on the light in her room. Then she straightens her clothes tidily, finds her Bible, and gropes her way hurriedly along the dark path toward the church.

The cigarette-store man, on the other hand, has nothing to do with the church. When the fourth chime wakes him, he rolls out of bed, lights the fire, and starts preparing for the day's work.

Now the fifth and the sixth chimes ring out, echoing through the village. These and all the rest of the chimes go to different houses every day. Sometimes they visit the elder's house, and sometimes they visit the house of Pyongchan, the Sunday-school student. To be perfectly honest, they do whatever they please. They ride around excitedly on the cool morning wind, and wherever they feel like it, they go into a house and wake the family.

But there's one person the chimes almost never reach. Grandma Guema is always complaining that she never hears them, even though she lives in the middle of the village. At first, the chimes blamed themselves for this and rallied together to try harder. But the real problem is that Grandma's house is tucked behind a ridge in a deep part of the valley. Although the chimes fly as far as they can, they usually flop down partway, too tired to go on. Even when they get to Grandma Guema's house, by the time they tap on her ear they are so weak that they sound like someone eating runny porridge. To make it worse, Grandma Guema is deaf, and she sleeps very soundly.

That's why the people in the church eventually agreed that something had to be done. In the end they bought Grandma Guema an alarm clock as a gift from the congregation. Otherwise she would hardly ever wake up in time for morning prayer, despite being a true believer in Jesus.

On a few days each year, though, the *Deng!* of the chimes reaches even Grandma Guema. That happens when the wind is blowing exactly right. On those days, the chimes travel on and on, over the mountain to the neighboring village of Tangdang-gol. They arrive in the village exactly together with the whistle of the early-morning train. When the children in Tangdang-gol hear the chimes and the whistle together, they are so excited that they talk about it for the rest of the day.

Every morning then, the bell ringer for the church on the hill pulls the bell rope – down and up, down and up – and the chimes ride out on the morning winds to all the houses. But they don't just visit the houses where people live. They also go to the homes of the owl, the magpie, the wild boar, and the wolf.

When the chimes visit the wolf, he's so lazy that even though he badly needs to pee, he just keeps lying there snoring loudly. Only when he hears the chime does he open his eyes, stagger to his feet, and slowly relieve himself. Afterward he lies straight back down to sleep again.

The wild boar opens his eyes. The father magpie opens his eyes. The other animals also open their eyes. Then they all decide that it's still too early and go back to sleep.

Although the bell ringer always tries to count how many times he rings the bell, he often gets confused. Sometimes he rings sixty-one times, sometimes sixty-five times, and once he rang seventy-one times. Although he doesn't know it, the owl is in the oak tree listening to him every day, keeping count. Since the owl has been up all night, he's always wide awake and can count the exact number of chimes.

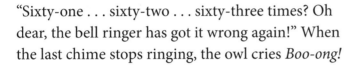

"Sixty-one . . . sixty-two . . . sixty-three times? Oh dear, the bell ringer has got it wrong again!" When the last chime stops ringing, the owl cries *Boo-ong!*

Some days the bell ringer oversleeps. Then the owl flies over the roof of his house crying *Boo-ong! Boo-ong!* The bell ringer leaps up, startled by the owl's hoot, and sees that he's already five minutes late. Barely pulling on his trousers, he dashes out and starts yanking on the bell rope. The owl alights on the roof of the bell tower and calls to him: "Bell ringer, if you had gone on sleeping it would have been a disaster!" Then the owl takes wing, flying back toward his home on the mountain.

The bell ringer gratefully calls after him, "Thank you, Owl, thank you!"

It's in this way that the chimes fly out every day without fail to the stars in heaven, to the village, and to the mountain peak. And so the people, the animals, and the birds all become one family. When the chimes ring out, the windows of the church on the hill shine brightly, and the people from the village gather there and sing beautiful hymns to praise God.

Today the chimes from the church go especially far, as far as Tangdang-gol. They fly over the mountain, ringing brightly to wake the sleeping villagers.

They swoop down from the sky and chatter like little angels to announce a new day. It's a day for living kindly and honestly. It's a day for giving thanks to God.

THE END

The Church I Dreamed Of

Against Christian Idol Worship

KWON JEONG-SAENG

Many years ago I told a friend I wanted to start a church. It wouldn't have a big steeple with a cross on top; I'd just build a traditional Korean pavilion-style house just large enough to hold fifty or a hundred people. No pulpit, just a wooden floor where we could sit in a circle. We wouldn't have a sign out front advertising "So-and-so's Church" either. We'd call it "The Magpie's House," or name it after a fairy-tale character.

At our church services, we'd just talk about our lives and the Bible. Sometimes a monk might come over from the temple and read from Buddha's teachings, or the schoolmaster might tell about Confucius and Mencius. On special days like Dano, the rice-planting festival in early summer, we'd roast a pig, share home-brewed rice wine, dance, and play games. When hard times came, we would help each other. That's the kind of church I wanted.

This idea filled me with enthusiasm, and I prayed about it. But years passed, and the church was never built.

I've been a baptized Christian for thirty years, serving as a deacon for much of this time, but I've never been to a service that fully satisfied my longing; often the ritual seems empty of real life. Nevertheless, I think I met God when I lived in a little room by the church door and rang the morning bells. I still miss the peace I felt on cold winter mornings when I pulled on the bell rope and looked up at the brilliant stars in the black sky.

Back then, in the 1960s, the early morning prayers at the village church were simple and beautiful. The memory of kneeling to pray on the cold wooden floor by the light of an oil lamp – there was no electricity – seems sacred. The church members were poor. They had all lived through bad times, and their talk was spare and honest. One deaconess had lost her husband in the war and lived with her only daughter. It used to tear my heart to hear her sing her favorite hymn: "I follow God's will amid this world's joys and pains, and when my body fails, give me great faith."

Then she would break down sobbing and

Kwon Jeong-saeng (1937–2007) grew up as a refugee of the Korean War, during which he contracted tuberculosis. Even later in life, after his children's books met with commercial success, he continued to live in a small and simple one-room dwelling near the bell tower of his village church, which he served as deacon and bell ringer (see his story "The Bell Ringer" on page 50). Having himself suffered wartime violence and poverty, he became a passionate advocate for children victimized by war; at his death, he left all his lifetime savings to children in need, especially those in North Korea. This essay, written in 1996, was translated from Korean by Raymond Mommsen; it appears here in an abridged version.

everyone would fall silent. After the service was over and everyone went home, the sun shone in the church windows and you could see the frozen marks of tears on the wooden floor.

We were all poor, but the church was full of love. If you would flip through the church account books from those days, you might see when a few hundred won from the church fund were lent out to a parishioner in need.

Back then, the pastor's salary was barely enough to live on, sometimes only a bushel of millet and a few baskets of rice. To repair the derelict church building, he had to go into the mountains and fell trees, and for water he had to dig his own well. As a result, it was easy for him to become close to his parishioners. In the evenings, the young people would gather in the church foyer to weave baskets and read together. They worked until late at night and then roasted sweet potatoes and turnips. Most people had no money to put in the collection plate; their offering was to donate their work and show love. In this way, Christianity simply became a part of people's lives.

It was an isolated mountain village of about fifty families, in which the church had first arrived a hundred years earlier – only a few thatched huts and a tin-roofed church. But it almost felt like heaven on earth. There was no theft, nobody drank or smoked, and nobody yelled or cursed. Unlike elsewhere in Korea, we never suffered the "barley famine," the weeks in spring before the first barley harvest when people used to starve, since each household had enough farmland to supply itself with food.

This way of life ended abruptly in the 1970s, when the church succumbed to authoritarianism, materialism, and religious emotionalism. Instead of praying quietly in their hearts, people yelled and babbled like lunatics. No longer was it a matter of duty and vocation to serve as elder or deacon – instead it became a position of status and power. Big-city pastors discriminated against village pastors, and churchgoers discriminated against one another, growing cold and distant in their relationships. People still smiled and greeted each another, but they no longer spoke honestly and sincerely. Their Christianity changed from a faith that depended on God into a religion aimed at attaining power, money, and success – using God as a convenient instrument. If you didn't become rich within three years of accepting Jesus, people thought there was something wrong with your faith.

The big revivalists even distorted the Korean language, saying words like "believe," "accept Jesus," and "love" with such slurred pronunciation that you could hardly understand them. Was it a gift of the Spirit that made them talk that way, or just boundless arrogance? Even swindlers selling fake medicine don't talk so sloppily. Didn't the apostle Paul say that love is not arrogant or proud? Jesus said that you should pray in secret, that you should comb your hair and not put on a show in front of other people when you fast, that your right hand shouldn't know what your left hand does. He warns against babbling in the marketplace.

But what do many churches do? They go all over the world shouting and yelling and then call it mission; aren't they really dishonoring God? The church is in danger of becoming just another pollutant, spreading trash instead of salt and light. But too many Christians don't pause to think; they carry on without realizing the true state of affairs, just like the proverbial emperor in his new clothes.

"You will know a tree by its fruits." How is materialistic, success-driven Christianity helping our society? Are all the red-neon crosses you see in our cities the true light of the church? Our country leads the world, true enough – in alcoholism, sexual assault, car accidents, and hellish academic pressures. Our "mission" consists in bragging about our per-capita national income. Meanwhile we've buried our mountains and rivers in trash and filled the city sky with smog. We need to come to our senses and stop trying to deceive God. The Christianity spread today is like the food sold in the markets, full of poisonous chemicals and nicely packaged. We must stop using Jesus' name to sell fake Christianity.

I just described my Christian village in the mountains, but not everything there was good. Wherever Christianity came to a village, our traditional culture was destroyed – stamped out as superstition and idol worship. We Christians gave up our beautiful customs and adopted Christmas as our main holiday, going crazy over Santa Claus, Rudolph, Christmas trees, and Christmas cards.

I don't deny that traditional culture included bad customs as well as good. But can it be right to reject all aspects of a culture that has shaped our souls for tens of thousands of years? God is present even without Christianity; he doesn't need churchgoers in order to work. Whether or not a country is Christian, God reigns. He has ruled the universe for countless ages. The missionaries think that God depends on them and their preaching – that he trails after them, staying only where they have been. But long before Christianity was preached, God watched over the whole world. People may not have known him with their minds, but their hearts could feel him.

I remember when my friend Pan-son's mother was alive. Once her next-door neighbor, a woman who had just had a baby, was starving. Pan-son's mother took rice from the urn in the dragon god's shrine and cooked it for them. The rice in that jar wasn't just for the dragon god, but saved the lives of dying people – a miracle.

Similarly, it used to be a common custom that when a family member went on a long journey, the family would fill a bowl of rice for them at every meal. That food was served to any wayfarer who came unexpectedly; even the poorest houses never sent visitors away hungry, and better-off households always kept a room empty for travelers. People working in the fields who sat down for lunch would call out to a passerby inviting him to share their meal.

Calling these customs superstition and idol worship profanes something sacred. The apostle Paul said that even faith that moves mountains is nothing without love. You can travel the whole world on evangelization campaigns, building churches with thousands of members, but it's nothing if you don't love people. Even if you memorize the Bible, heal thousands of sick people, or get a doctorate from a first-rate seminary, it's nothing if you can't show love in the commonplace ways.

Korea's churches need to relearn these lessons. If we rediscover the true gospel of Jesus, not the Westernized gospel, we will find the breath of God. We'll see that he has been working in our country ever since he created the world.

Years ago I dreamed of building a new kind of church, but actually that misses the point – the whole universe is God's church. My only wish is to live uprightly within it together with all nature – human beings, animals, and plants – each serving the other. This is what God wants; this is why he sent Jesus to earth. Jesus taught us to love by serving one another, and he shed his blood and died for this. The real idols and real demons in our land are imperialism, war, nuclear weapons, dictatorship, and violence. ⇒

Christianity's Third Divorce

ELIZABETH STOKER BRUENIG

Deep Church Rising: The Third Schism and the Recovery of Christian Orthodoxy
Andrew G. Walker and Robin A. Parry
(Cascade, 194 pages)

For a modestly sized book, Andrew G. Walker and Robin A. Parry's *Deep Church Rising* surprises with its broad historical imagination. The authors pose an urgent question: how is Christianity to cope with a world increasingly hostile to its message and mission? They suggest that Christians' polarized responses to that question will lead to schism, the third in a series of schisms to have divided the Christian world. The first was the "Great Schism," the splitting of East and West that divided the church into its Greek and Latin branches. Then came the Protestant Reformation, further fracturing Western Christianity. And while these two divorces are still keenly felt, Walker and Parry argue that a third is on the way – one that positions apostasy against orthodoxy, and in so doing cuts within branches and denominations rather than between them.

Walker and Parry – both seasoned theologians – detect the early symptoms of this third schism among Christians who have fallen under the influence of "versions of modern Christianity which, although modern, are not Christian." These weakened strains of Christianity, they contend, undercut a trinity of truths without which the faith can't endure: right belief, right worship, and right action. The result? They see a growing tendency within all Christian denominations to view religion as basically private and personal, a matter of individual therapeutic preferences rather than a response to objective truths. There's a corresponding quickness to re-imagine Christian ethics in ways that force the faith into compliance with a utilitarian world. For example, Walker and Parry note that "more than a few liberal Christians take it as obvious that a pregnant woman has a straightforward right to choose whether or not to carry her child to term." And this is only one of many disturbing shifts away from historical Christianity – the authors do not meditate long on others, but they are not hard to imagine.

Taken together, these developments have sowed confusion as to what it is that Christianity teaches. The "family resemblance" left over by the first two schisms is therefore seriously threatened by this third.

Deftly tracing the roots of the cultural context that has produced the third schism, Walter and Parry take the reader on a whirlwind jaunt through early Christianity, the medieval period, the Enlightenment, and through to modernity. Though this excursion might leave some readers dizzy, it serves a necessary purpose. By drawing on thinkers ranging from Augustine, Tertullian, and Anselm to Locke, Kierkegaard, and Kant, the authors are actually modelling their suggested solution to the third schism: a return to tradition.

It's the care with which Walker and Parry issue their call that makes *Deep Church Rising* so persuasive. "Deep church," a phrase borrowed from C.S. Lewis, refers in part to "a common historical

Urbino Bible, ca. 1478

tradition of belief and practice that was normative for Christian experience." That is, "deep church" means a set of truths about belief, worship, and action which remains constant for all Christians, everywhere and always. These truths, the authors argue, are the stars by which we can set our course, regardless of where we find ourselves in human history. It so happens that much of Christianity's best charting was laid out before the modern era, by Augustine, Aquinas, Gregory, Irenaeus, and other teachers. Walker and Parry point out that the reasoning of ancient and pre-modern Christians was not (as is now often suggested) rooted in superstitions and cultural norms long past their use-by date. Far from being a product of sociological accidents, tradition is the fruit of the apostolic church's journey through history.

While the authors admit to being "traditionalists or primitivists of sorts," *Deep Church Rising* is not anti-modern. Rather, it declines to accept modernity as the standard by which Christians should define their faith at all, whether pro or con. "It should go without saying," they write, "that [a *Deep Church* sensibility] is no threat to science, only to scientism, the ideology that all truth claims about the world can be assessed by the sciences." The answer to modernity isn't to collapse backwards into the lifestyle of a bygone time, but rather to develop a robust Christianity that is both orthodox and capable of grappling with today's problems.

In true traditional fashion, this begins for Walker and Parry within the church herself. Their concluding two chapters suggest how this might look: through renewed attention to teaching the faith ("Recovery of Catechesis"), and through a deepened reverence for the Lord's Supper ("A Eucharistic Community"). They describe the "Eucharistic community" as the hub that gathers all Christian doctrine together; here we gather to share in "a meal for the time between times; to taste the life of the age to come." Reflecting on the Eucharist allows Walker and Parry to do three things: to expose the "gospel amnesia" that has corroded Christian orthodoxy; to remind us of the strong, elegant theology that modern Christianity has largely forgotten; and to sketch out the ecumenical project they have in mind for the future. This chapter beautifully illustrates the authors' vision of belief, worship, and action as indivisible.

Walker and Parry don't hold out the false hope that the trajectory of secular thought will be interrupted anytime soon. Yet they refuse to give up any ground, even when that means taking deeply unpopular positions – it's difficult to imagine a harder sell to the average millennial Christian than Saint Augustine on sexual morality. Like the ministry of Christ itself, the quest to recover a deep church is demanding but not violent, hard but not merciless – its essential purpose is the achievement of unity. For the authors, this means a unity with multiple layers: of the present church with the tradition that precedes her; of today's schismatics with orthodox believers; and of the whole body of Christ brought into communion through the Eucharist.

Readers interested in a renewal of orthodoxy and a clear-eyed vision of what a deep church might look like will be grateful for this thickly argued and rewarding book. It includes two helpful appendices: an essay on the Nicene Creed and a critique of fundamentalism. The authors do not hold to a literalist reading of the Bible, nor do they believe that such a "neutral" or "obvious" interpretation is even possible. But their defense of a broader-minded interpretation is compelling, and – thanks to the authors' commitment to taking scripture seriously and traditionally – may pleasantly surprise readers with more literalist convictions.

With its richness of detail and wide-ranging theological vision, *Deep Church* is a fine book to read slowly. It's also well suited for reading in discussion groups – there's plenty here to fuel much-needed conversations.

Elizabeth Stoker Bruenig is a writer born and raised in Fort Worth, Texas, now pursuing a doctorate in religion from Brown University.

Finding the Balm in Gilead

Lila: A Novel
Marilynne Robinson
(Farrar, Straus and
Giroux, 272 pages)

Balsam trees growing
in the Gilead highlands
above the Jordan River
once yielded the balm
of Gilead, a healing resin used, in the words of
an old spiritual, "to make the wounded whole."
The Gilead of Marilynne Robinson's novels is a
fictional Iowa town described as "a dogged little
outpost." It's a humble setting for the playing out
of great themes – redemption, faith, innocent suffering, and love – in a manner that resonates with
modern readers. Writing in *The New Yorker*, Mark
O'Connell notes that, "She makes an atheist reader
like myself capable of identifying with the sense of
a fallen world that is filled with pain and sadness
but also suffused with divine grace."

Robinson's *Lila*, appearing this autumn, is her
third novel in a row to share the Gilead address.
(Her debut novel, *Housekeeping*, has a different
location and sensibility.) The first of the three
books, *Gilead* (2004), won the author a loyal
readership and a Pulitzer Prize. Its central character, John Ames, is an elderly preacher who has
married a younger woman, Lila; the book is a
letter he writes to their son, whom he knows he
will not live to see grow up. The letter weaves
together his recollections with pieces of fatherly
advice ("This is an interesting planet. It deserves
all the attention you can give it"). He reflects on his
ancestry or "begats," including a fiercely abolition-
ist grandfather who fought with John Brown. (In
a subplot, uneasy race relationships continue to
haunt the 1950s Gilead that Ames inhabits.) The
book's dynamic heart is John Ames himself – wry,
as honest as he is able to be, and open to joy. In his
words, "Grace has a grand laughter in it."

Home, published in 2008, tells the same story
from the perspective of Glory, a Gilead native who
has returned to take care of her dying father. Told
by an omniscient narrator, *Home* lacks *Gilead's*
warm resonance – like other readers, I found
myself missing the presence of John Ames.

Now *Lila* provides the backstory to *Gilead* and
Home, tracing the orphaned Lila's childhood with
a ragged community of vagrants who are eventually separated by the Depression. Lila struggles
on alone until the day she wanders into Gilead.
Her early history is told in fragments, alternating
with the story of her arrival in town, John Ames'
shy courtship, and the growth of her love to him.
Their relationship is complicated by her wariness
of a repose she knows will be temporary, given his
age. The novel's best passages are the conversations
of this odd couple as they negotiate their engage-
ment, start a marriage, and wait for their child. He
is bemused and pleased by her efforts to become
a preacher's wife by copying grim passages from
the Old Testament to teach herself to read. ("You
know," he remarks to her, "I wouldn't mind if you
were reading Matthew, along with Ezekiel. Just a
suggestion.")

Lila repeatedly replays her painful childhood
and youth, both in her thoughts and in their
conversations. Her sense of the "bitterness and
fear" of existence runs up against John Ames's
faith in redemption. Those who loved *Gilead* will
appreciate hearing the story from the viewpoint
of a woman suspicious of cheap grace. But readers
new to Robinson may be best off starting with the
earlier book.

Lila ends with its main character seeing a
vision in which all the broken men and women
she has known arrive in heaven to be welcomed
and comforted. She resolves to share this vision
with her husband: the promise of the true balm in
Gilead. ➵ *Eleanor Land*

Digging Deeper · *A Justice Reading List*

Start talking about justice, and you can quickly find yourself mired in competing definitions and agendas. The following books will help readers toward a deeper understanding of justice in light of the gospel.

Must Reads: Nicholas Wolterstorff's *Journey Toward Justice: Personal Encounters in the Global South* is a marvelous encapsulation of his work. Wolterstorff writes as a first-rate philosopher on the basis of his own experiences in South Africa, the Holy Land, and Honduras, combining a thorough grounding in scripture with a lucid style. He argues that justice doesn't make sense without a robust view of rights: those in need have certain morally binding rights on those with the ability to help. Highlighting the priority that justice enjoys in the Bible, he debunks attempts to mute its demands by showing how integrally it is connected to love, mercy, beauty, and peace.

Rich Christians in an Age of Hunger by Ronald J. Sider has become a modern classic in Christian social responsibility. Rightly so: the book is a creative synthesis of biblical, social, and practical commentary that convicts and inspires at the same time. It's indispensable for anyone who wants to know what the Bible teaches about justice and the poor and is willing to take a hard look at his or her own life. Sider pulls no punches in his call for concrete action, yet he also thoughtfully addresses complex realities such as structural injustice, international debt, multilateral corporations, and global warming. Though the statistics in the fifth edition (2005) are outdated, the wisdom and passion of *Rich Christians* remain as relevant as ever.

Eberhard Arnold's *God's Revolution: Justice, Community, and the Coming Kingdom* is a powder keg – a collection of short readings that spell out what it means to live out the justice of God's kingdom. (For a taste of Arnold's writing, see his essay on page 12.) The author situates the demands of God's justice within the context of practical, shared community that foreshadows the coming future of God. In this way, justice is more than a moral requirement or ethical ideal; it is a re-envisioning of our world and the church in accordance with the gospel. An introduction by John Howard Yoder places Arnold's work and life (1883–1935) in their historical context.

Camille Pissarro, Woman Digging

Recommended: While Wolterstorff, Sider, and Arnold give broad treatments of justice, Charles Avila's *Ownership: Early Christian Teaching* has a tighter focus: wealth as understood by the early church. Avila surveys what ownership meant in the Roman world before turning to the thought of Clement of Alexandria, Basil, Ambrose, Chrysostom, and Augustine. In gathering together extracts from their sermons and writings addressing wealth, Avila arrives at some startling conclusions. For a start, his survey demolishes the common assumption that Christianity views private property as a natural or absolute right. Simply as a collection of quotations from the church fathers on a crucial topic, this excellent and provocative book deserves careful reading.

The United States has less than 5 percent of the world's people, yet nearly 25 percent of its incarcerated population. *Beyond Retribution,* by Christopher Marshall, and *Changing Lenses,* by Howard Zehr, are two books that explore how this happened and what we can do about it. Marshall's book is a scholarly treatment of biblical teaching on justice and retribution, whereas Zehr's lays out a new, truly Christian approach to criminal justice practice. Both authors see God's justice less as a matter of punishing evildoers and more as long-suffering love that overcomes evil with good, repairs the damage done by sin, and restores human relationships. ➤ *The Editors*

Must Reads

Journey toward Justice
Personal Encounters in the Global South
Nicholas P. Wolterstorff
(Baker)

Rich Christians in an Age of Hunger
Ronald J. Sider
(Thomas Nelson)

God's Revolution
Justice, Community, and the Coming Kingdom
Eberhard Arnold
(Plough)

Recommended

Ownership
Early Christian Teaching
Charles Avila
(Wipf & Stock)

Beyond Retribution
A New Testament Vision for Justice, Crime, and Punishment
Christopher D. Marshall
(Eerdmans)

Changing Lenses
A New Focus for Crime and Justice
Howard Zehr
(Herald Press)

Once in the West: Poems
Christian Wiman (Farrar, Straus and Giroux, 128 pages)

We were hard-pressed to settle on one poem from this forthcoming collection to include in this issue (see page 19). It's not just the apt metaphor – a skipping stone, a bee beating the glass, "one tatter-demalion dandelion / adrift in the air / like happy ash." Nor is it Wiman's way with words: where the perfect modifier is needed, he's not afraid to conjure a new one – try "stabdazzling darkness, icequiet." No, Wiman is one of our favorite poets because his work is suffused with an authentic, hard-earned faith, where one can find the sacred in a desert or an alley, fraternity in a road crew or a rest home, and doubt and assurance in the same breath. Wiman, a former editor of *Poetry* magazine who now teaches at Yale, has been battling cancer, so the wistful, elegiac mood running through many of these poems comes as no surprise. Nor does the recurring theme of prayer:

> I said I will not violate my silence with prayer.
> I said Lord, Lord
> in the speechless way of things
> that bear years, and hard weather, and witness.

Silence Once Begun: A Novel
Jesse Ball (Pantheon Books, 256 pages)

In this ingenious new novel set in Osaka Prefecture, Japan, eight old people vanish from their homes without a trace. In a wager at cards, a twenty-nine-year-old thread salesman named Oda Sotatsu agrees to sign a confession taking responsibility. At that moment he takes a vow of silence which he maintains throughout his imprisonment, trial, conviction, and execution. But why? In the absence of the central character, our narrator, a foreign journalist named Jesse Ball, is left to piece together conflicting accounts from Sotatsu's family and associates. Who is telling the truth? Whose truth?

Clever in its construction, but devastating in its implications, this is more than a commentary on the limits of criminal justice. Ball dedicates the book to Kobo Abe and to Shusaku Endo, whose profound 1966 novel *Silence*, filled with the silence of God and the fickleness of man, finds an echo here. And unmentioned but never far away is the innocent Jesus standing silent before Pilate, or before Dostoyevsky's Grand Inquisitor.

The True American
Murder and Mercy in Texas
Anand Giridharadas (W. W. Norton, 336 pages)

Proving that real life can be as compelling as the best fiction, Giridharadas, a *New York Times* columnist, tells the intersecting stories of Raisuddin Bhuiyan, a Bangladeshi immigrant working in a Dallas minimart, and Mark Stroman, a red-blooded American who seeks to avenge 9/11 by shooting foreigners at gas stations. Ten years later, Bhuiyan, the only survivor of the shootings, is moved by his Muslim faith to show mercy to his attacker, and even campaigns – unsuccessfully – to stay Stroman's execution and free him from death row. With attention to detail and admirable empathy for both his subjects, Giridharadas traces the making of these two men and their efforts to rebuild their lives. Which is the true American? We are forced to reflect on the possibility that both are.

No Irrelevant Jesus
Gerhard Lohfink (Michael Glazier, 342 pages)

This is a wonderfully readable collection of loosely connected reflections from a first-rate New Testament scholar, each casting light from a different angle on Lohfink's underlying insight: that discipleship is never a solitary affair. On the personal level, the author reveals his own journey toward Christian community in a fascinating and challenging account that causes the reader to take stock of his or her own faith. Combining academic acumen with an accessible style, Lohfink addresses such perennial questions as: How does Jesus' death actually save world? What are we to do with Christ's fragmented body? How are we to relate to those of different faiths? In what sense is the gospel good news for the poor? This book offers a full meal to savor on one's own or to feast on with others. ➢ *The Editors*

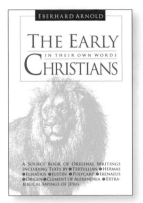

Recommended Reading

The Early Christians edited by Eberhard Arnold. What did Christianity look like before it became an institution? As Plough's founding editor, Eberhard Arnold, writes, "At that time a fresher wind blew and purer water flowed, a stronger power and a more fiery warmth ruled." This vibrancy lives on in these writings of our common spiritual ancestors, pointing us back to the wellspring of our faith. Topically arranged primary sources include Origen, Tertullian, Polycarp, Clement of Alexandria, Justin, and Irenaeus. Revealing material from pagan detractors and persecutors is included as well. *"This selection will not only help readers understand early Christianity intellectually; it will also challenge them to live more fully, abundantly, and even radically." – Justo L. Gonzalez*

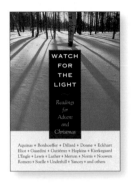

Watch for the Light (anthology). While there are many Lenten devotionals, the other great spiritual season, Advent, is often lost in the bustle of Christmas preparations. With selections from the world's great spiritual writers and poets – Dietrich Bonhoeffer, Annie Dillard, C.S. Lewis, Thomas Merton, Kathleen Norris, Henri Nouwen, T.S. Eliot, Gustavo Gutierrez, Dorothee Sölle, G.M. Hopkins, Edith Stein, Thomas Aquinas, and Philip Yancey, to name a few – this book will help you center on the true meaning of the season: the coming of Christ into our midst and his promise to return. *"Born of obvious passion and graced with superb writing, this collection is a welcome – even necessary – addition to glutted holiday bookshelves." – Publishers Weekly*

Jesus and the Nonviolent Revolution by André Trocmé. In this classic work, Trocmé, the French pastor famous for hiding Jews during the Nazi occupation, explores the "politics of Jesus" and shows the ongoing relevance of his ethic of nonviolence and justice. Trocmé writes, "All of us, Christian and non-Christian alike, are responsible for the hunger, injustice, egoism, and wars that devastate our time. Christians bear special responsibility: knowing that God can change both people and their situations, the disciple of Jesus can help bring into being God's future for humanity." *"This book deserves to be more widely known. Trocmé's focus saves any account of salvation from pietistic distortion." – Stanley Hauerwas*

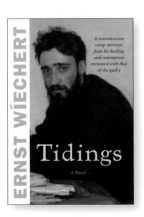

Tidings by Ernst Wiechert. Like the author, who spent four months in Buchenwald concentration camp for opposing the Nazis, the characters in this novel, both victims and perpetrators, seek healing and redemption as they return home after the war to pick up the shattered pieces of their lives. First published in German in 1950, *Tidings* deserves its place among the masterpieces of European literature. *"Romantic in feeling, mystical in outlook, spendthrift in prose . . . Wiechert presses home his message with intense sincerity." – Time Magazine*

www.plough.com
Free access to dozens of e-books for* Plough Quarterly *subscribers.

Heaven in Hell's Kitchen

Saving Manhattan, One Child at a Time

EIRLYS HINE

It's a sunny afternoon in late May. I'm standing on West 51st Street and 10th Avenue in Manhattan, shifting an over-stuffed duffel bag from hand to hand. The bag contains all the worldly possessions of my good friend, Danisha, who fled from her apartment yesterday with only her baby and the clothes on her back.

Walking down the street, I fight off a sense of irritation. I know I am going to be late to a class I can't afford to miss. The bag is heavy, I am somewhat lost, and it is going to take me at least half an hour to get to school after this. Impatiently, I walk down the sidewalk, looking out for the Sisters of Life Sacred Heart of Jesus Convent, where I am hoping to find Danisha. I've been told that this convent has sheltered hundreds of women since its founding, accompanying mothers through the birth of more than 150 babies. I am expecting something imposing and grand.

Instead, after ten minutes' search, I set the bag down on the doorstep of an unassuming, homey building surrounded by trees and tended gardens. I ring the bell and try to look in a hurry.

Minutes pass. As I wait, I remind myself of what I've read about the sisters and their work.

Sister Loretta works in the Sisters of Life's house in Manhattan.

Founded in 1991 by John Cardinal O'Connor, the order's mission is straightforward. In addition to the traditional monastic vows of poverty, chastity, and obedience, the Sisters of Life take a fourth vow promising to protect and enhance the sacredness of every human life.

This fourth vow shapes the sisters' sense of vocation. Sister Bethany Madonna, for example, joined the order at the age of twenty-five just because of it – she felt she was called very specifically to help vulnerable mothers-to-be. She is one of seventy-seven sisters in total, whose average age is thirty-five, far below what is usual for American Catholic orders. They live in and staff four convents in the United States and Canada that provide safe havens for women in a "crisis pregnancy" or seeking healing after an abortion.

While my friend was neither of these – her baby was nearly a year old and fiercely loved and wanted – she needed somewhere safe to go. "Of course she is welcome to stay with us," the Sisters of Life had said when my pastor called them. It didn't matter that Danisha's case didn't fit their mission exactly. They took her in then and there.

Today all I have to do is deliver Danisha's belongings. When the door finally opens, I have a thirty-second excuse prepared explaining my errand and why I simply cannot be late to my class. The woman in the doorway dissolves my impatience with a beaming smile, and I forget

my speech. We exchange greetings and then I am inside, following her down a narrow hallway until we come to a door with a simple, hand-written sign stuck onto it: "Welcome Danisha."

In the room, I find my friend cradling her son, her eyes blurred with tears. I am at a loss for words and ashamed of my hurry. Dropping the bag, I give my friend a hug and search feebly for something encouraging to say. When I tell her finally that I have brought "all her stuff," she manages a dramatic eye-roll.

After we run out of words, we sit on the bed and watch the baby laughing at the shadows on the wall. The fact that Danisha has taken refuge with the Sisters of Life along with her child makes her something of a special case for a convent used to sheltering women who are pressured to have an abortion. Forty-one percent of pregnancies in New York City end in abortion. The numbers are even higher among minority women. Yet while saying, "Abortion is wrong!" is necessary, it's also too easy. As I watch Danisha with her baby I consider how few of us are willing to give active, concrete support to even one of the millions of women whose pregnancy creates a crisis for them.

The Sisters of Life provide practical and spiritual support to hundreds of these women. Mothers can stay at the convent for up to a year after the birth of their baby; they are able to develop personal relationships with the sisters, attend prayer services and mealtimes, and receive the food, clothing, and items necessary for raising a child. Most of the women come from abusive or impoverished backgrounds, and, like Danisha, lack a safe environment to return to. "One of the hardships and challenges of the mission," says Sister Grace Dominic, "is witnessing the fear and distrust that can often overwhelm and deceive women."

That afternoon, however, nothing on the face of the sisters who come through Danisha's room, "just to say hello," betrays discouragement. It's rare that a person really looks radiant; the sisters do. "We are mindful of our complete dependence on God for everything in our lives," is Sister Grace's explanation. Donations provide everything they need to run the mission, including all items needed for the new babies. After all, didn't Jesus promise that his Father would give good gifts to those who asked him? By embracing the poverty of the women they work with through their own vow of poverty, the sisters are able to identify with them in a way that many other nonprofits would simply be unable to do.

I can feel this solidarity as I sit with my friend and her baby in the sunlit room with the handwritten sign of welcome. I'm not glancing at the clock on the wall anymore. Why am I always so frantically racing from one thing to the next? What has Danisha taught me with her humility and her patience? What can I learn from the way these sisters have sacrificed their own wishes and dreams to help found a place here in Hell's Kitchen, in the heart of Manhattan, where my friend can find solace and comfort?

Eirlys Hine studied education at City College in Manhattan. She is a high-school English teacher in Nonington, England. Meet the "contemplative/ active" community of the Sisters of Life at www. sistersoflife.org.

Isaiah

JASON LANDSEL

"I heard the voice of the Lord, saying, 'Whom shall I send, and who will go for us?' Then said I, 'Here am I; send me.'" (Isaiah 6:8 KJV)

So began the mission of a man who loved his country, cared for his people, and sacrificed his life for God's reign of justice. Sometimes called "the Shakespeare of the Bible," he is among world literature's greatest poets. Severe toward tyrants, compassionate toward the disadvantaged, and expectant for God's intervention in history, Isaiah gives voice to the cry for justice by oppressed peoples still today.

The prophet whose name means "The Lord is salvation" lived seven centuries before Jesus' birth. After receiving his divine vocation, Isaiah worked tirelessly for sixty years, rebuking the people of Israel for putting their faith in military power and political alliances and urging them to trust in God alone. With his wife, called "the prophetess," he had two sons whose names were themselves a prophetic message: Shear-Jashub means "a remnant will return," while Maher-Shalal-Hash-Baz means "quick to the plunder, swift to the spoil." Willing to do anything to convince the people to repent, he walked Jerusalem's streets "naked and barefooted" to illustrate what would happen if God wasn't obeyed (Isaiah 20:3).

When I began work on a portrait of Isaiah (see opposite page), I needed someone to pose as the prophet. My longtime friend Larry Mason immediately came to mind. Larry's life has been full of struggle and hardship from childhood on. He fought in the Vietnam War as an E6 staff sergeant in the 101st Airborne and First Cavalry Divisions, serving three consecutive tours and seeing intensive combat. Years later, he took a pilgrimage back to Vietnam to pay his respect to the Vietnamese

people for their losses and to seek healing from the wounds of war. Now Larry considers himself a soldier in God's army. He is an example of turning swords to plowshares, and he has dedicated the rest of his life to living out the Sermon on the Mount in full Christian community.

Knowing Larry's love for Isaiah's prophecies, I asked him how he thinks they apply now. His answer: "When I look around at today's world, I often pray the Aramaic prayer for the early return of Christ: 'Maranatha – O Lord, come!' I read in the news about the craziness of man, the shootings and wars, the corruption of politicians, the greed of big business. Hardworking people so often don't stand a chance. Then I think of God's promise: 'Behold, I make all things new!' (Rev. 21:5)

"A lot of what Isaiah prophesied is still going to happen: God will 'create new heavens and a new earth' (Isaiah 65: 17–25). So we all better get off our butts and be prepared, because God's kingdom is coming very soon! As I sit with my morning coffee in front of the house, I often look to the sunrise where we are promised there will be signs in the skies of Jesus' return. 'For the Lord himself shall descend from heaven with a shout, with the voice of the archangel, and with the trump of God' (1 Thess. 4:16–17). Then Isaiah's vision will finally become reality."

Jason Landsel lives in Rifton, New York with his wife and three children. He is the contributing artist for Plough Quarterly's *"Forerunners" series, profiling courageous men and women of faith through the ages.*

"And it shall come to pass in the last days, that the mountain of the Lord's house shall be established in the top of the mountains, and shall be exalted above the hills; and all nations shall flow unto it. They shall beat their swords into plowshares, and their spears into pruninghooks: nation shall not lift up sword against nation, neither shall they learn war any more."
(Isaiah 2:2, 4)

Jason Landsel, *Isaiah*

Saint Francis, the Artist

In 1940, Laurence Housman mused on the poor man from Assisi.

VEERY HULEATT

The pages of *Plough's* spring 1940 issue are yellowing, but the cover remains a rich maroon. The place of publication is Ashton Keynes, Wiltshire, England, the price is one shilling sixpence. Feature articles respond to the six-month-old conflict soon to be known as World War II: "Christians and the State," "Quakerism and War," "Christ or Civilization." Grouped uneasily with these war-time reflections is a poetic essay on Saint Francis by Laurence Housman.

Although overshadowed by his more famous brother, *Shropshire Lad* poet A.E. Housman, Laurence Housman was himself an accomplished author – his *Little Plays of Saint Francis,* with its memorable portrayal of the holy fool Brother Juniper, remain a minor classic. Yet writing was only Housman's second vocation. Before his eyesight failed, he had worked as an artist, providing intricate Art Nouveau–style illustrations for the 1893 edition of Christina Rossetti's *Goblin Market.*

During his long career as a public intellectual, Housman dedicated his talents to promoting the ideals which he believed in, including socialism, pacifism, and women's suffrage. At the Quaker meeting he attended, he became close friends with Dick Sheppard, the founder of the Peace Pledge Union. Together with other British pacifists including Vera Brittain, Aldous Huxley, and Benjamin Britten, he became a sponsor of the organization. *Plough Quarterly* exists today thanks in part to Housman's generosity: he supported the publishing house financially after its 1937 expulsion from Nazi Germany.

"Saint Francis, the Man," the 1940 essay Housman wrote for *Plough,* muses on Francis as "one of the most alive people that the world has ever produced":

> Had he been by nature a painter or a poet, Saint Francis might have joined the immortals on a lower scale than that which he attained; and might, from a worldly point of view, have lived a more contented life, expressing his sense of beauty – the beauty of holiness – in a more attainable form of art than that which he made so strangely his own. But though we hear on one or two occasions that he drew, and that when he took up a craft in the early days of the Brotherhood he chose woodcarving, we have no reason for thinking that he did these things specially well. His "Canticle of the Sun" is spiritually beautiful and expressive, but it is not great art. The artistry of Francis lay in another direction; he was the instinctive dramatist, the play-actor; and with this gift went another – an extraordinary power of imaginative sympathy, which made him a wonderful reader and manipulator of human nature. . . .
>
> Were all artists like him, our duty towards our neighbor would become a game. He played it so beautifully that the memory of how he played it is still with us – a possession for the meek upon the earth.

Detail from Henri Martin, *Saint Francis of Assisi*

PAST AND PRESENT

St. Francis, the Man